D1605548

BUYING LAND

Other books by the author

Dollars and Sense: A guide to mastering your money
How to Avoid the Ten Biggest Home-Buying Traps
Making Money in Mutual Funds
The Home-Owner's Survival Kit
The Complete Book of Home Remodeling,
   Improvement and Repair
Building or Buying the High-Quality House at the Lowest Cost
How to Judge a House

A. M. WATKINS

Buying Land:

HOW TO PROFIT FROM THE LAST GREAT LAND BOOM

QUADRANGLE / The New York Times Book Co.

The graph on page 62 is copyright © 1970 by Coldwell, Banker & Company.

Copyright © 1975 by A. M. Watkins. All rights reserved, including
the right to reproduce this book or portions thereof in any form.
For information, address Quadrangle/The New York Times Book Co.,
10 East 53 Street, New York, N.Y. 10022. Manufactured in the
United States of America. Published simultaneously in Canada by
Fitzhenry and Whiteside, Ltd., Toronto.

Design by Emily Harste

Library of Congress Cataloging in Publication Data

Watkins, Arthur Martin, 1924-
    Buying land.

    Bibliography: p.
    Includes index
    1.   Real estate investment—United States.   I.   Title.
HD255.W34   1975   332.6'324'0973   74–24283
ISBN 0–8129–0531–8

CONTENTS

PREFACE

Investing in land can be a risky business. The trick, of course, is to do it wisely rather than foolishly, a trick that may seem considerably easier to accomplish than it actually is. Consider, for example, the stories of three men I encountered while doing research for this book.

One man who made a wise investment in land is John C. Lincoln, whose story is told at the beginning of Chapter 1. During the 1930s Lincoln bought large tracts of Arizona desert land for as little as $1 an acre. After World War II, he found that his land had soared in value to $15,000 to $20,000 an acre! It is worth even more now.

Another wise investor is Don Carter (not his real name), who is an expert at buying and selling land. Land investment has given him a splendid home in the United States, a handsome apartment in London, and a sprawling ranch in Guatemala. Always on the lookout for good land, Carter may buy some for a couple of thousand dollars an acre, more or less, or maybe $10,000 to $20,000 an acre. Within a few years, he will sell it at four or five times that value, if not more. He has done this a number of times in the past twenty years. How he did it recently, turning a $25,000 cash investment into a $90,000 profit in little more than a year, is described in chapter 8.

Then there is poor Joe Katman (also not his real name), who has never learned the trick of successful land investment. Nevertheless, hope springs eternal with Joe. In the past twenty years he has bought approximately twenty different parcels of land. He has bought land the way other people buy antiques, figuring he was casting his bread on the waters. But in Joe's case the bread has never returned, much less returned tenfold. He still owns almost all the land he has bought. He can't sell it today except at a loss, and in some cases a considerable loss. In short, he's stuck with a lot of land. He can do little with it but continue paying the yearly tax bills, or else give it up.

For every John C. Lincoln or Don Carter who buys and sells land wisely, making a handsome profit, there are probably ten to twenty Joe Katmans who invest foolishly, or unthinkingly, and who suffer the consequences. They include people who venture miles from home to buy country property, many of whom buy it as an investment, as well as a place for a second home. They also include those who have swallowed the deceptive propaganda that you can't lose investing in land because it's an easy road to riches.

Now, land can indeed represent a splendid opportunity for investment, whether you buy solely for financial reasons or for the dual reason of a place to live that will also be a good investment. Moreover, the value of *certain* land will surely be driven up higher in value in the future than ever before. Overall, however, investing in land will be far more perilous in the future than at any time in the past.

Today, land investment has become a whole new ball game, because of three suddenly converging forces—(1) the tide of new environmental controls and restrictions over land use that is sweeping the country; (2) the spate of slow-growth and no-growth laws being passed by more and more communities; (3) the energy crisis. In addition, it is beginning to dawn on a growing number of people that the United States is now approaching a time when its population growth will hit zero. No new land will be required then for an expanding population because the population will no longer be expanding.

In sum, the whole land game is undergoing drastic changes. More than ever before the importance of buying land wisely and intelligently cannot be overemphasized. This brings us to the purpose of this book—to report the effect of radical social changes on land values and to tell you how to shop for and buy land wisely and intelligently.

The following chapters set forth the fundamental principles that have almost always been followed when people have invested successfully in land. They were followed when John Jacob Astor bought land on Manhattan Island and founded his family fortune; they were followed when Marshall Field, the Chicago department-store tycoon, made a second fortune buying and selling land ahead of Chicago's northward growth; and they were followed when John Lincoln, Don Carter, and other people you never heard of also did very well for themselves investing in land. Conversely, the very same essential principles were ignored when many more people like Joe Katman invested in land unsuccessfuly.

There is nothing secret about these essential principles. Professionals in the business use them all the time. They involve such considerations as how growth patterns develop in an area, good timing, and how to obtain highest and best use. Many actual examples showing how professional investors employ such principles when they buy land are given in the chapters that follow. Obviously, how it's done in practice can hold lessons for all of us, amateur or professional.

The seasoned professional investor also offers us much guidance in other areas that can cause problems when a person enters the market for land. A few examples:

•   The minimum appreciation rate of land required just to break even. It used to be that land need only double in value within seven years, but that minimum rule of thumb is now as obsolete as the five-cent candy bar.

•   The best ways to buy and finance land. It is usually, though not always, with the lowest possible cash down payment.

•   The usual strategies employed by the people who are the most likely sellers encountered when you follow up land for sale.

•   And the different ways to buy land. You might do it all by yourself, with another person or two in a joint venture, or in a one-time syndication. Each has its advantages and special drawbacks.

There are, of course, other things to know about land when you think you might have a little fling at it, or a big fling, if you will. I have tried to embrace all of the most pertinent and relevant facts and to present them here comprehensively and succinctly. Much effort has also been made to give you these helpful facts in clear, simple, and understandable English. It is the strong intention of the author to please as well as inform.

A. M. Watkins

BUYING LAND

chapter 1

THE LAST GREAT LAND BOOM

In 1931 a Cleveland inventor and industrialist, John C. Lincoln, became enchanted with the Arizona desert and moved his family to Phoenix. He settled in a distant northeast part of the town and soon began buying up all the desert land he could put his hands on, paying as little as $1 to $3 an acre.

In the years following World War II, the area he chose, Paradise Valley, became the most fashionable address in Arizona, if not in the whole Southwest and his cactus-covered land sold for $15,000 to $20,000 an acre. Not bad for a beginner.

There was still good opportunity to do well in land a quarter century after Lincoln had staked out his first cheap claims. If you had bought $10,000 of farmland ten years ago, it would be worth about $24,450 today, based on the average rise in value of all farmland in the United States in the past decade, according to U.S. government figures.

If you had put $10,000 into two or three home-building lots ten years ago, your land would have tripled in value by now, based on the average increase in residential land in the past decade.

If ten years ago you had bought choice commercial land in the growth path of an outlying metropolitan area for $10,000, it would be worth about $40,000 now, based on the recent 15 percent increase in value per year for such premium land.

You would have profited most of all, however, if you had put your $10,000 into a few top-notch acres at the location of a future superhighway interchange. After the highway bulldozers had come and gone, your land today would very likely be worth from $50,000 to $200,000 for a really desirable site. If an oil company, for example, had wanted part of your land for a gas station at a corner of the interchange, you might have sold a slice of less than an acre for about $75,000 to $80,000, the recent going price for such sites.

The value of land should soar even higher in value in the United States in the future. Not all land, however, will increase in value, and not everyone will do well buying land in the future, just as not everyone has done well investing in land in the past, despite all the stories—and books—written about how to make a fortune in real estate. Let us immediately put to death the hoary and mistaken cliché that goes, "You can't lose with land because God only made a certain amount of it." More on the demise of this idea later.

To be sure, John Jacob Astor founded one of the great American family fortunes nearly two hundred years ago in New York City by speculating in cheap Manhattan farmland just ahead of a period of rapid growth. But Astor had it relatively easy. For one thing, Manhattan is a long, thin island and the city had been established on its southern tip; future growth inevitably had to move north and only north. All Astor had to do was "Buy on the fringe and wait," but there was in the main only one fringe to gamble on. For another, even Astor hedged. He occasionally dipped into the wide hip of Manhattan to buy a radish patch or two on the Lower East Side. But land values there never subsequently approached the astronomical values of other Manhattan land he had bought to the north, including the corn farm he bought that later became Times Square. Not all land speculators of the time, however, were as successful as Astor. Many other people bought land and lost out. Robert Morris, the Revolutionary War hero, for example, lost a fortune speculating in land and died a pauper's death in debtors' prison.

Today there are also "more losers than winners in the land game," in the words of Albert Winnikoff, a professional land investor in southern California, one of the experts I sought out and talked with during the research for this book. Winnikoff wrote about his experiences with land in *The Land Game*. (Facts about his book and other recommended sources of information on land are given at the end of this book.)

That's true now as well as yesterday, even in gold-coast areas where land supposedly never stops climbing in value. New York City, for example, is the location of some of the most highly prized, most valuable land in the world. Many people besides Astor have over the years made money in Manhattan land, but not everybody. "It's not generally known that the larger part of Manhattan land is today priced below its value of the 1920s," says Daniel Friedenberg, a New York real estate man whose family has been investing in Manhattan property for more than fifty years.

And in Chicago people frequently mention how Marshall Field, the department-store founder, made a second fortune speculating in land ahead of that city's northward growth. But not many mention

There is far more land in the United States than will conceivably ever be needed, and much of it can be used for more than one purpose. Energy transmission lines, for example, run below this lovely vista. (*Courtesy Atlantic Richfield Company.*)

the hundreds, if not thousands, of others who lost money in Chicago's half-dozen classic boom-and-bust land cycles since 1830. While Field played it cool in the early 1870s, for example, there was one James H. Walker, a real estate tycoon who ran his land and real estate holdings up to a reported value of $15 million dollars, a sum worth close to $100 million in 1970 dollars. He and countless others were wiped out by the panic of 1873.

Land prices can go down, as well as up, as shown by what happened after that panic. Within a few years the average value of all land in the sprawling, brawling adolescent Chicago of the time dropped by an average of more than 50 percent, according to Homer Hoyt, the professional dean of American land and real estate economists, and author of the classic book *One Hundred Years of Land Values in Chicago*. But that's just the estimated average drop. Choice land downtown on Michigan Avenue that had sold for $1,000 a front foot in 1873, was four years later going begging for $200 a foot. Land to the north that had been selling for $3,000 an acre was driven down in value to a mere $375 an acre.

Three main reasons for successful land investing

On the other hand, nearly every person who has bought land and later sold it at a nice, if not resounding, profit was successful because of one or more of the three main reasons that underlie nearly all profits made with land. He was just plain lucky, a highly common reason. Or he had that indefinable, intuitive feeling that enables some people to sense valuable land in the making. Or third, he chose land at the right place, which means in an area of growth, and pretty soon spreading growth of a city or suburb caught up with his holdings and made them more valuable than before.

By no means do I downgrade the first two reasons, but it is the third reason—how to narrow your choice to land that is most likely to be in the path of growth and therefore to rise in value—that is at the heart of this book. It's at the heart of all intelligent buying of land, not just for investment profit, but also if you seek country property for a vacation place or retirement home. As a matter of fact, knowing well this third reason also contributes to what others call luck, and also to having that ingrained sense of land values.

Knowing how to buy land in the path of growth, then, obviously calls for a little knowledge about how cities and towns spread and grow—in short, the basic patterns that almost all growth follows. You will also do well to know about the crucial importance of timing when you buy or sell land, and how the value of land and the price that it goes for is inexplicably linked with its "highest and best use."

Why new demand for land?

Such knowledge will be virtually indispensable in the future because the buying of land in the United States has suddenly become far more risky and treacherous than at any time since the first great land boom before Astor's time. We are, to be sure, heading for still another great land boom in a long cycle of them, this one sparked and fueled by that bumper crop of "war babies" born in the 1940s and 1950s. With the force of a tidal wave, they inundated our grade schools in the 1950s and swept through bulging high schools and colleges in the 1960s. Now they are getting married, having children of their own and entering the market for houses—and land—in record numbers, as shown in detail in the next chapter. Their mothers and fathers spawned the boom in the 1950s when they left our cities en masse and marched out to suburbia to create countless Levittowns and unparalleled suburban growth.

Unlike that last boom, and nearly all others before it, the next great eruption in land values will be riskier than ever before, partly because of the energy crisis, which will probably be with us for some time, and largely because of strict new controls being put over land for ecological reasons and environmental integrity.

The energy crisis has already put a brake on rising land values in many a suburban area and country region. Not only does nobody yet know how much reduced energy supplies will curtail travel and settlement of the land in such areas. But also no one knows how we will build all the new power plants and find the necessary energy to fuel such future growth.

New controls over land

As for ecology and environmental controls, no one in his right mind today can buy land without considering them, whether you wish merely to pitch a tent, or to build a modest house, or to plan a

STANDARD METROPOLITAN STATISTICAL AREAS OF THE UNITED STATES AND PUERTO RICO: 1970

ALBERS EQUAL-AREA PROJECTION

U.S. DEPARTMENT OF COMMERCE

Greatest future growth in the United States should occur mainly in these areas closest to the 250 largest metropolitan areas.

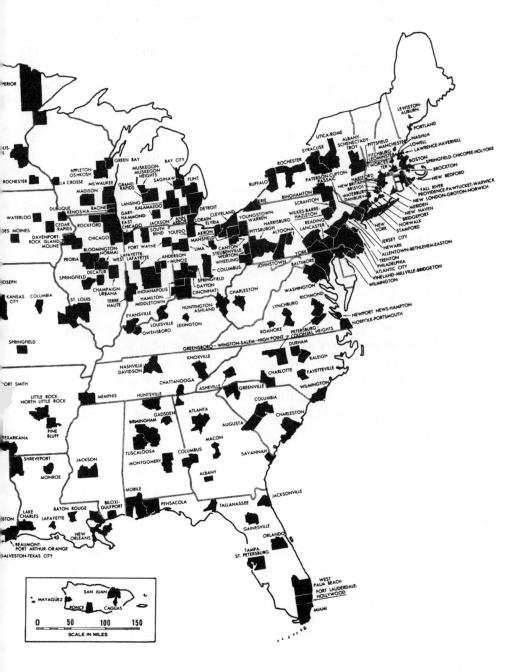

BUREAU OF THE CENSUS

multimillion-dollar development of one kind or another. In California, for example, I was told of the young doctor who had bought a $14,000 lot high over the Pacific Ocean north of San Francisco. It was to be the site of his dream house for his wife and family. The local environmental protection agency objected, however, and blocked construction on his land. It was ruled that a house there would not be in the public interest because "it would obstruct the ocean view of passing motorists"!

In Oxnard, in southern California, the Larwin Group, a large real estate developer, was stopped in its tracks from developing new housing on a large tract it owned there. Local government officials put the land in "an open-space land bank," with no building allowed on it till 1990. The market value of the land consequently plummeted from $8 million to $4 million. California has long been the pacesetter state in such restrictive legislation trends; among other things, its voters also passed a tough 1972 referendum putting stiff controls over the use of all land within 1,000 yards of its 840-mile shoreline.

At last count some one dozen states, in all, had passed land-use control laws of one kind or another and others were debating such new laws. Vermont, for example, imposes a stiff capital gains tax on short-term (up to six years) land-sale profits to discourage speculation and the uncontrolled growth that can follow. The more quickly land is sold, the higher the tax. In 1974 a national land-use law was being given serious consideration by the U.S. Congress and eventually some form of it may be passed.

No growth and slow growth

More and more cities and large and small towns are getting into the act. Three mushrooming suburbs of Washington, D.C., found that their sewer systems were overloaded and acted in understandable fashion. They declared building moratoriums that banned new construction until their sewer systems could be expanded and lines extended out to new growth areas. Not unexpectedly as a result, land values in the areas dropped by 20 to 30 percent within a short period, I was told by leading brokers there. The moratorium also prompted a Washington radio announcer to quip that you no longer make a fortune in land by following the highways; now it's "Follow the sewer lines!"

Other communities are instituting slow-growth policies that put a severe if not total brake on the new building allowed within their boundaries. The purpose, of course, is to give a community a chance to catch its breath and provide the new services required for the new building already in place. That, too, is understandable, if not always legal. Home builders and developers fought such a controlled-growth law in the Town of Ramapo, New York, some forty miles northwest of midtown Manhattan. They were rebuffed, and the slow-growth law was upheld by the state's highest court.

A constitutional question emerges

Now comes the sticky problem: besides the question of the wisdom and overall fairness of such laws—some may be and others not—there is the question of their legality. Such laws, as we've noted, serve, in effect, to take a person's property from him, even though he remains the owner of record. Yet the Fifth Amendment to the U.S. Constitution says, "private property may not be taken for public use without just compensation." That's the rub, and its many ramifications may take a long time to be resolved by the Supreme Court.

Besides, there are two sides to the coin. On the one, many environmentalists and others are understandably reacting to more than a little misuse, abuse, and sheer rape of the land by greedy fast-buck operators, developers, and others whose dirty work has hurt everyone.

On the other side, it's also true that some overzealous defenders of the environment have clearly gone rather far in lashing out at almost anyone with plans to use land. In Tucson, Arizona, for example, vigilantes, striking at night, vandalized a builder's new housing to the tune of a half-million-dollars' worth of damage. Finally caught, they turned out to be four architectural students from the University of Arizona who had turned outlaws to save the land, or so they said.

Now, obviously, we can neither allow butchery of the land on the one hand nor singleminded, overzealous opposition—or destruction—to any and all new development on the other hand. A middle ground is clearly needed. What's more, there's no reason why growth and development cannot exist side by side with care and consideration for ecology and our environment. The thesis of this book is that both are possible, simultaneously, though it may be necessary to curb a few reckless practitioners on both sides of the issue. How else are we ever to provide the desperately needed new housing and other facilities for our underprivileged people, and for old people of limited means, not to mention the deprived, ordinary middle-class families also seeking new houses and apartments in growing numbers?

The huge demand for such growth and development clearly must be satisfied for the good of all of us. It's also pretty clear that new land-use laws and controls, and just plain honorable respect for our environment, are here to stay. And they have introduced a whole new inescapable element in the game for nearly everyone who will buy land from now on.

The environmental revolution is also a major reason why the land boom abuilding is likely to be our last great land boom. Within the next decade or so a whole new set of inevitable land-use codes and controls will almost certainly emerge. As in Europe, they will put a damper on the buying and selling and use of land freely and indiscriminately in the future, as we have known it in the past.

Zero population growth

Even more important, perhaps, our long history of land booms and growth cycles in the United States is due to grind to a halt within the next ten to fifteen years because the supply of land will catch up to what will then be diminishing demand for it. Like a high spring tide,

Land Required to House 1 Million People
for Various Residential Types

Type of units	Number of acres
High-rise	4,474
Medium-rise	6,734
Garden	15,037
Townhouse	20,964
Single-family	111,111

More multi-family housing will be built in the future than in the past. Because it requires less land for an equal number of people than does single-family housing, comparatively less land will be required in the future for housing. And housing is by far the largest gobbler of all of land. (Source: September 1971 *Urban Land*, reprinted with permission of The Urban Land Institute, 1200 18th Street N.W., Washington D.C. 20036.)

the present surging demand for land will almost certainly be followed by a spring ebb. Demand will fall off sharply because, for the first time in our long explosive national history of virtually uninterrupted population growth, zero population growth is looming closer and more clearly on the horizon. In 1971 the U.S. birth rate turned downward and hit a record low within a short time. It will evidently continue at a low annual rate, if not decline more, according to demographers, the people who keep track of such things.

These experts foresee actual net zero population growth in the

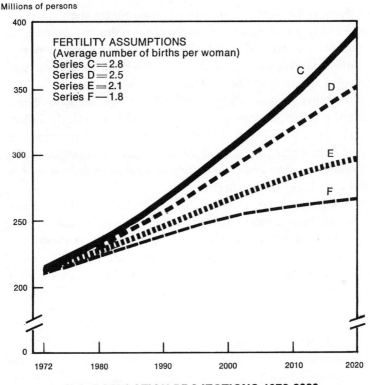

Millions of persons

FERTILITY ASSUMPTIONS
(Average number of births per woman)
Series C = 2.8
Series D = 2.5
Series E = 2.1
Series F — 1.8

U.S. POPULATION PROJECTIONS 1972-2020

U.S. population in the early 21st century could hit anywhere between 250 and 400 million people, depending on the birth rate between now and then. Population projections for the future are based on four of the most likely birth rates, according to the Bureau of the Census, and the results are above. In the early 1970s, the rate fell below 2.0 babies per 1,000 women, the lowest in decades.

United States in the year 2040, give or take a decade or two. That's the year, in other words, in which they now figure that the national birth rate, death rate, immigration rate, and other such ebb-and-flow numbers will come into balance. And then the U.S. population will no longer grow. But just as Wall Street's players discount stock prices in advance of future economic developments, so will land prices be discounted and very likely discounted well in advance of our actual descent to the zero population level.

More land than we need

Besides, there is far more land in the United States than we could ever conceivably use, despite the continual cries that we are running out of land. Not counting the vast Alaskan tundra and huge reserves of government land stocks, there are still more than five acres of land per person in the United States. Much of it is more accessible and usable than many people think. That will be increasingly so if new mass transit systems, now being discussed and planned, do indeed pan out. They could fan out from cities and succeed in bringing large portions of distant peripheral land into the active market for usable land. At one swoop the available supply of land in an area would be expanded by a logarithmic increase.

Even within our larger cities, from 12.5 to more than 22 percent of the total circumscribed land area consists of vacant lots and unused tracts. As much as one-third of all private land is vacant and unused! That's according to a study not long ago by the National Commission on Urban Problems, shown in Table 1–A. Look around as you drive through almost any suburban community and you may be amazed at all the vacant land, not to mention underused land.

In sum, a surging new demand for land is building up in the United States, and it will generate an unprecedented land boom across the country. But it will be a far more selective boom than ever before. For those who will buy land, it will be far more risky, difficult, and potentially explosive boom than before. There will be more and more court battles and controversies, if not outright civil war, fought between those who wish to buy and use land and those who will fight their right to do so to the last ditch. More land-use controls will be born and given legal sanction. All of these forces converging will make much land unusable and banked away, driving down its value

Table 1–A   Land use in U.S. cities, 1966

Type of land use	102 Cities over 100,000 population*		40 Large cities over 250,000 population**	
	Percent of land area	Acres per 1,000 population	Percent of land area	Acres per 1,000 population
Totals	100%	130.1	100%	97.5
Public streets, roads	17.5%	23.0	18.3	18.2
Privately owned land:				
Residential	31.6	44.3	32.3	37.0
Commercial	4.1	5.4	4.4	4.6
Industrial	4.7	6.1	5.4	5.7
Railroads	1.7	2.2	2.4	2.3
Vacant	22.3	26.9	12.5	11.9
Total private land	64.4%	84.9 %	57.0 %	61.5 %
Public and semi-public (excluding streets, roads, parks, other recreational schools)	4.9%	5.6 %	5.3 %	4.6
colleges	2.3	3.2	1.8	2.1
Airports	2.0	3.1	2.5	2.9
Cemetaries	1.0	1.2	1.1	1.0
Public housing	.5	.5	.4	.4
Miscellaneous uses	3.0	2.2	5.1	2.9
Total public land, less streets	13.7	15.8	16.2	13.9
Total public and private land, less streets	82.5%	108.3 %	81.7 %	79.3

*Out of 130 such cities in the United States in 1960 and includes the 40 large cities, next column
**Out of 52 such big cities in the United States in 1960.
Source: the 1968 report of the National Commission on Urban Problems from its Three Land Research Studies, Research Report No. 12, 1968 (available for 70¢ Government Printing Office, Washington, D.C. 20402), and in this from "Land Use in 106 Large Cities," by Allen D. Manvel. Figures in each column do not add up to exactly 100 percent because absolute data for each use for all cities was unobtainable.

and reducing the available supply. At the same time they will drive up the value of other available land to very high levels.

That's the picture shaping up for the immediate, foreseeable future, which will be a convulsive period. It will also be your last chance to participate in a great land boom if only because we as a nation simply will not stand for any more such convulsive periods afterward. And mostly because of other converging forces, consisting of the imminence of zero population growth, and the growing realization that we really have more land available than we will ever need. Besides, new rapid transit and mass transit systems can bring that land into the mainstream of urban and suburban use quite easily.

Incidentally, the approach of zero population growth should by no means bring a cessation of economic growth and improvements.

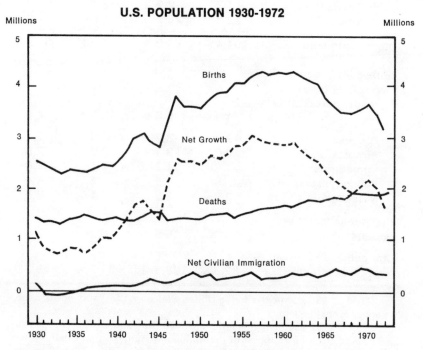

U.S. POPULATION 1930-1972

Millions

Births

Net Growth

Deaths

Net Civilian Immigration

Here are the major forces that determine the overall population. Note how the birth rate slumped to a longtime low in the 1930s, rose sharply after World War II, then began declining again. (*Bureau of the Census.*)

Table 1–B   Average value of U.S. farm land since 1910, dollars per acre

Year	Value	Year	Value
1910	$40	1943	38
1911	41	1944	43
1912	42	1945	47
1913	43	1946	53
1914	44	1947	60
1915	43	1948	64
1916	46	1949	66
1917	49	1950	65
1918	53	1951	75
1919	58	1952	82
1920	69	1953	83
1921	65	1954	82
1922	57	1955	85
1923	56	1956	91
1924	54	1957	97
1925	54	1958	103
1926	52	1959	111
1927	50	1960	116
1928	49	1961	118
1929	49	1962	124
1930	49	1963	130
1931	44	1964	138
1932	37	1965	146
1933	30	1966	158
1934	31	1967	168
1935	32	1968	179
1936	32	1969	188
1937	33	1970	195
1938	33	1971	203
1939	32	1972	219
1940	32	1973	249
1941	32	1974	310
1942	34	1975	357 (Estimated)

Source: U.S. Department of Agriculture

It should mean greater opportunity and greater emphasis on improving the quality of our goods and products for living, and emphasis on satisfying the soul, as well as our many material needs. In short, it can mean production for a higher quality of life, to use the current cliché.

Before we plunge into how to buy land wisely and intelligently in the last great land boom, you should first understand how the basic demand for land is generated and grows. And you should also know how current population currents will put different pressures on the future demand for land, compared with the past.

chapter 2

THE NEW DEMAND FOR LAND

Population growth, the phenomenon of more and more people occupying an area, is of course the key to growing demand for land, as any economist will tell you. It has less to do, however, with the number of new babies being born at the time—that is, the birth rate —than with the number of new grownups.

The great land and housing booms in sunny Florida and Arizona in recent decades were caused by people streaming into areas with pleasant climates. Sunny California also had a great post-World War II land boom, the granddaddy of them all. In recent years, however, the California land boom has gradually subsided, virtually parallel with the decline in the large annual influx of immigrants, which is now down to one-third of its former high rate.

For whatever reasons, when great numbers of people move into an area, a land boom inevitably follows. This has been true in the past as well as the present. It occurred repeatedly in our frontier towns of the West during the 1800s when numerous people of various interests—adventurers, cowboys, prospectors, entrepreneurs— descended on a new town with something special going for it and ignited a land boom, or a mini-boom at least.

The key to housing demand

The principal force contributing to increased national demand for land today stems from the "family formation rate," the economists' term for couples who get married and set up new "households" (though today there may be many households formed without the blessing of legal marriage). Such a couple, however joined, enters the market for a house or apartment; especially if it starts raising a family, the couple will need a larger place, including more land. Such people in their twenties and thirties historically have accounted each year for by far the greatest single group of home buyers. Their numbers have for some three decades exceeded the supply of available housing, so new land has had to be found to build the new houses they have needed. That's what happened in the 1950s when those millions of young men returned from war, got married (when formal marriage was in vogue), and started families. They moved en masse to the suburbs because that was where land was available for new housing.

As I noted earlier, it's due to happen on an even larger scale in the next decade because of that record crop of World War II babies in the last generation, though history may not repeat itself in exactly the same way. It's coming in one way or another simply because the number of Americans aged from 25 to 34 will increase in coming years by about *40 percent,* compared with the same number of same-age people in the United States during the 1960s, according to the U.S. Bureau of the Census. That's a greater bulge of people entering the market for housing than ever before, and they are precisely the people who have long accounted for the greatest number of U.S. home buyers each year.

Future demand

Those figures are no secret to experts who keep track of such things and have seen it coming for some time. For example, a 1970 study by Dr. Herman Miller and economist Roger Herriot of the Bureau of the Census predicted that U.S. expenditures for new housing would climb from $68 billion in 1968 to $168 billion by 1985, a whopping increase of 172 percent. That will be the second largest percentage jump for all U.S. family expenditures in that period, the first being money spent for personal and medical care (up 185 percent from $46 billion to $131 billion in 1985). Dr. Miller's predictions are shown in Table 2A. Though these projections were made in 1970, Dr. Miller told me later, in 1974, for this book that he would make no significant changes in them.

According to Mike Sumichrast, chief economist of the National Association of Home Builders, a total of 17 million new houses, apartments and mobile homes will be needed in the United States from 1975 to 1980 to keep up with the steadily mounting national demand for housing. That's an average of more than 2.8 million new housing units a year. It's more housing built each year than ever before in a single year. Top housing volume during the 1950s housing boom was a record (for then) of only two million new houses built in any one year, 1955.

The actual production of new housing in the country from 1975 to 1980 may not come up to Sumichrast's projections because of problems that may hold back housing production. The problems could result because of insufficient mortgage capital to finance that much new housing of insufficient energy to build them. Nonetheless, the demand for housing will continue to grow simply because of the

Table 2–A   Consumer Spending Patterns 1968 vs. 1985

Aggregate Current Consumption Expenditures of all Families and Unrelated Individuals (Billions of 1968 dollars)

Expenditure Category	1968	1985	Percent increase
Food, beverage, tobacco	$97	$174	79
Clothing and clothing materials	39	76	95
Transportation	60	124	107
Household operation and furnishings	63	132	110
Recreation, education, contributions, and other	59	147	149
Housing (shelter)	61	166	172
Personal and medical care	46	131	185
Total, all categories	$425	$950	124

Source: Herman P. Miller: "Tomorrow's Consumer" March 1970.

people who are coming of age and entering the market for housing. That will mean extra demand for housing—and land—spilling over into the 1980s.

Any skeptic still with doubts about the mounting demand for new housing should be told that other experts confirm the growing pressures for new housing. A study by Harvard and MIT's Joint Center for Urban Studies, for example, predicted that some 2.3 million conventional houses and apartments will have to be built each year for the rest of the 1970s, plus another half million or more new mobile homes to take up the slack.

If such great demand has been building up for new housing,

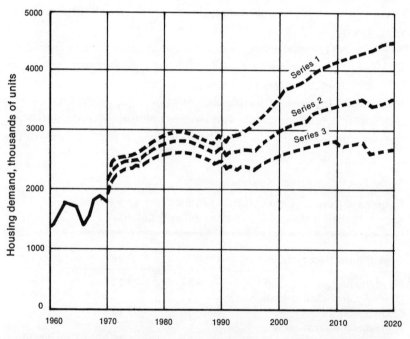

Total demand for housing, 1960-70, with projections to 2020

Housing projections can be much more accurate than population projections because housing needs, are based on people already born. The key is what economists call the formation of households, which in regular English means the number of people getting married. Above housing projections needed are based on the Bureau of Census' low, medium and high assumptions (Series 1, 2 and 3) of the future marriage rate. (Source: Michael Sumichrast, Chief Economist, National Association of Home Builders.)

Table 2–B   Estimated housing needs for the 1970s (in thousands)

	Net increase in U.S. families	Total annual demand for new housing	Total new housing units
1970	1,222	2,160	1,864
1975	1,430	2,551	2,725
1976	1,478	2,640	2,775
1977	1,538	2,720	2,825
1978	1,480	2,691	2,875
1979	1,450	2,697	2,920
1980	1,430	2,687	2,950

why has the home-building industry been rocked by major slumps, as in 1974, a disaster year for new housing production? Home building also slumped sharply in 1969 and 1970. It was because of tight-money policies during both those periods when the government, via the Federal Reserve System, choked up on the national money supply. Interest rates soared to more than 12 percent for prime corporate borrowers in 1974. Very little money was left for banks to lend as mortgages to home buyers at even 8 or 9 percent interest rates.

It was a classic tight-money situation on a national scale. And when builders cannot borrow money to build and sell houses they stop building houses, which is what happened. Sales of used houses slumped even worse than sales of new houses. Two to three used houses are generally sold each year for every new house built and sold. The same sort of national tight-money crunch not only cut down sharply on new housing production in 1969, but also in 1966, in 1959, and off and on before then. It will probably recur in the future, causing big disruptions in the industry and major problems for consumers (such as forcing up house prices), until government officials and politicians in Washington get smart and prevent this vicious cycle.

Yet the demand for new housing can continue to grow even though few new houses are being built and fewer houses, new and old, are being sold. People continue to get married in record numbers and require more housing. Many, however, simply are compelled to put off buying a house for a while, as they did in 1969 and 1959. They buy later, as they did in 1971 and 1972 when home sales soared in greater than expected numbers. So, just because housing may go through a periodic slump, as in 1974, it doesn't always mean that the demand for houses has slackened. Virtually all indicators point to a record, sustained demand for new housing at least until the middle of the 1980s.

"The Birth Dearth"

What is not necessarily understood, however, is that the *kind* of new housing built in the future could be considerably different than the traditional housing that we know from the past. And new trends in housing could mean new trends in land use and land values. For one thing, houses will be smaller and more compact in the future than in the past because of the "birth dearth," says Washington, D.C., economist and demographer Ben J. Wattenberg, author of the book, *The Real America.* Putting it another way, he says, "Enter the two-child American family, exit the three."

It started in the first six months of 1971, he says, the year when with little fanfare the U.S. birth rate dropped to its "lowest level in all American history—a level ten percent lower than during the years of the Depression!" Some demographers may be unsure that this new low-fertility rate will last, but Wattenberg says "enough indicators indeed suggest otherwise." Then came the 1973 figures showing that our birth rate had continued to fall and then hit the lowest annual rate ever, 2.1 births per 1,000. A birth rate of 2.17 per 1,000 women is the break-even point, the "replacement rate" needed to maintain present population.

Wattenberg concludes that the birth dearth will continue at least through the 1970s, because of such current factors as birth control ("the pill"), legal abortion, higher divorce rates, and changing social and religious values. "There will be more people in America in the years to come [because of steady immigrant flow to the United States] but not as many as [formerly] expected," he says.

In short, exit the four-bedroom house, enter the three. Houses are getting smaller and more compact. Because they require less land, you can look for more of the so-called town houses, garden apartments, and multi-family housing. As a matter of fact, the town house has become very popular. In recent years it has made up as much as 15 to 20 percent of all new housing built. Its roots stem, of course, from the old one-family row houses built downtown in colonial Boston, New York, and Philadelphia.

Much less land will be profligately gobbled up in the future by the traditional one-family house. In the booming 1950s, such houses, each set primly on its own private lot, accounted for roughly 90 percent of all new housing built and sold each year in the United States. But soon afterward their share of the market began falling sharply. By 1970 the traditional one-family houses made up less than 40 percent of all new houses and apartments being built each year.

End of the single-family house

The era of the traditional one-family house on its own private lot, row after row of them has, in fact, ended in America, except for people who are rich or who live in small towns and rural areas where land is still relatively cheap. The price of land in most metropolitan areas and suburbs has climbed so high that it is now out of reach of most middle-income families in need of new houses. Such land for a single-family house now costs from $10,000 to $15,000 per lot, if not more, in the typical large-city suburb.

Metropolitan land has climbed so sharply in value, moreover, that it constitutes about 25 percent of the selling price of the typical new house in suburban America today. A new house priced at $60,000, for example, breaks down in cost to roughly $15,000 for the lot and $45,000 for the house. Up to 1960 land generally accounted for only about 12 percent of the house sales price; in other words, only $7,200 for the improved, bargain lot that you got then with a $60,000 house. On top of all that, the cost of materials and construction labor for new houses has climbed since World War II at more than twice the annual rate of increase of all other items in the government's cost of living index. All housing has climbed steeply in price but the princely single-family house on its extravagant, outsized lot has clearly become the highest-priced luxury of all.

The mobile home steps in

To fill the vacuum for low-cost housing, the mass-produced mobile home has, while regular housing costs shot up, become more and more popular at bargain-basement sales tags. It is also having a decided impact on land use.

The mobile home won't win any Atlantic City beauty contest, and the appearance of many, though not all, mobile home parks, may leave something to be desired. Some of the new and modern parks are, however, quite attractive, set back from the road and screened from view by trees and fences. And despite the tin shoebox exterior of the typical mobile home, the interior is practically indistinguishable from a tidy, middle-income ranch house. Furthermore, the mobile home provides surprisingly large house value for the money. Where, three-quarters through the twentieth century, can you buy a fully equipped and furnished three-bedroom house with central air conditioning, less land, for as little as $10,000?*

As a result, mobile home sales, which were few in 1960, passed beyond the 400,000-a-year mark in 1970, and they are still rising. More than 500,000 were made and shipped in 1974, according to the last count. The federal government acknowledged in 1972 that the mobile home is here to stay when it began to include mobile home production in its annual figures for all new housing. Midway through the 1970s, about five million American families were living in mobile homes. And remember that most mobile homes are mobile only on their way from factory to site. Once at the site, the wheels of the typical mobile home are removed, the unit is lashed down, and is seldom moved again.

Roughly, half of all new mobile homes are set permanently on private land, mostly in small towns and rural areas. The other half are located in mobile home communities—usually called parks and mostly in metropolitan areas—with densities ranging generally from about six to twelve mobile homes per acre. That puts the price of land for mobile home parks roughly in the category of land for garden apartments of comparable density. The exact value of such land naturally will vary according to the number of mobile homes on it, the quality of the mobile home subdivision, and the land rent paid per unit.

As mobile homes continue to be turned out and sold to the tune of a half million or more a year, more and more land clearly will be sought for them and especially for the 50 percent or so that go into mobile home parks. The use of land for that purpose has become big business in a number of regions, particularly in the Midwest, Florida,

*Answer: Nowhere in America, in the world, except for a mobile home.

and the Southwest. It is almost certain to spread to other areas. Young married couples, by the way, are the largest single group of buyers of mobile homes, followed by retired couples.

Still another nonconventional and unexpected new kind of housing could well crop up in the future to fulfill the new demand for housing. For that matter, it could be tents, sleeping bags, or a new geodesic dome that will suddenly catch the public's interest and boom in sales as home buyers press for shelter. However the demand chooses to exert itself, it will almost certainly be expressed in a concomitant demand for increasing quantities of land, no matter what form the shelter takes.

Much land will also be required for new stores, shopping centers, offices, and the variety of amenities and services that automatically follow, like satellites, when new housing communities are built. Economists figure that for every dollar spent on a new house built and sold, another dollar is also expended for other economic activity stirred up. The sale of a $50,000 house sparks another $50,000, if not more, in sales of household appliances, furniture, furnishings, landscaping, and a variety of house and garden equipment and supplies needed to service new housing.

Where will all the land be chosen for such purposes, including that for new housing? Most of it, to be sure, will come in the path of future growth areas. This brings up the first fundamental principle for buying land wisely: how to determine future growth paths.

chapter 3

HOW GROWTH PUSHES UP LAND VALUES

Only an idiot will invest in land that is not in the imminent path of future growth. By that definition, though, many people who buy land to profit are idiots. It's not so much that growth may not come their way in the future. It is instead that the growth they expect approaches with glacierlike speed and, in fact, may never arrive during their lifetimes, and possibly not even in their heirs' lifetimes.

Consider, for example, how three different men chose to invest in land in one of the great growth areas of recent times, Arizona, but with varying results.

The first was John C. Lincoln who, as I mentioned earlier, bought land in a distant northeast section of Phoenix for as little as $1 an acre in the 1930s and found after World War II that his land had climbed sharply in value to as much as $20,000 an acre. He could not have chosen better. What special knowledge did Lincoln have? What made him choose so well, a barren desert land, largely unsettled, that was destined to climb in value?

While in Phoenix not long ago, I tried to find out why. Lincoln is dead now, but I sought out his son, Joe, who was a young boy at the time. Joe could not, unfortunately, shed much light on his father's motives other than saying that his father was intrigued with land in general and especially in the immediate area in the shadow of Camelback Mountain, including many high sites with a sweeping view of downtown Phoenix.

I concluded that Lincoln was in part lucky and in part endowed with some sixth sense that attracted him to an area that would later also attract other people with money. In addition, he helped establish the Camelback Inn, which later became a fashionable Southwestern resort for millionaire northerners. This exclusive inn also served to make his part of town, Paradise Valley, the most desirable address in Phoenix.

The second land investor there, whom I'll call Sam Ritter, was a native of Phoenix and a real estate appraiser. On a business trip to San Francisco in 1947 he was told by two American Telephone and Telegraph research economists that the population of Phoenix would double in the next ten years. Fired up by the prospect, Ritter returned home and began buying all the land he could. He chose to buy in the north and northwest part of town, paying up to several hundred dollars an acre. His son told me that his land rose in value over the next twenty years to $2,500 to $3,000 an acre, roughly a tenfold increase in value.

A principle to remember

That's not a bad profit for acting on the first rule of buying land: "Choose an area of growth." Ritter missed out, however, hitting it big by apparently not knowing another principle: "The highest land values in an area generally develop along a line outward from downtown toward the highest-income residential areas." In Phoenix this line ran directly out to John Lincoln's Paradise Valley, and then across the city line into Scottsdale where choice land today commands prices as high as $150,000 to $200,000 an acre.

The third player, whom I'll call Joe Phizzlewit, missed out completely. He made the common mistake of thinking that even in a major growth area you can buy land anywhere, anytime, and then sit back and let your profits mount. In 1959, he bought two hundred acres of land some sixty miles southwest of Phoenix for $300 an acre. It was one of the few places then where available land could be had that cheap. Joe threw darts at a dartboard, eyes closed, in effect, and also let the relatively low price of the available land influence him.

It was low priced because nobody wanted it, and nobody, in fact wants it today. Joe became disenchanted with his land in less than five years, and sold out for the best price he could get, a mere $75 an acre, thus a 75 percent loss. If Joe had used his brains, assuming he had any, and had done a little homework, he could easily have discovered more likely areas closer to Phoenix to invest in, especially then when the growth signs pointed to more and better land values developing farther out toward the northeast.

Historical patterns of growth

The first homework to undertake is an understanding of the historical patterns of city birth and growth. A quick review can be edifying. In the beginning, topography exerted a prime influence over the location of a new town and its subsequent growth, especially when defense from one's enemies was a major concern. The early Greek settlements were located for defense reasons each on an island or promontory, the Etruscan cities on hilltops; Athens was built near the Acropolis, Rome on its seven hills, Paris on an island, and London in the midst of swamps. Many, though not all, great cities were also located on or near a river, and those that were on or near the sea enjoyed particular advantages. Many great cities have also grown up at interior crossroads influenced by topography, as noted later.

Most of the great cities of the New World originated at the location of a natural harbor, protected from the sea, starting with the fine natural harbor of San Juan, Puerto Rico, first landfall of Columbus on his maiden voyage to America. Similarly the great cities of the eastern seaboard of the United States largely grew as a result of being endowed with good harbors. Such cities served as natural funnels for trade to and from the interior. An exception is Washington, D.C., whose site was, of course, deliberately chosen for its central location to the original thirteen states.

Why New York's supremacy

As it turned out, New York City later became the golden city of growth, far outdistancing such places as Boston, Philadelphia, and Baltimore. Early in the nineteenth century, however, New York did not have that much going for it. The reasons for New York's supremacy came shortly afterward. According to Richard M. Hurd, author of the classic book, published in 1904, *Principles of City Land*

Values: The Rise of Urban America, "The phenomenal growth of New York is due to there being but one topographical easy route from the West through the Appalachian Range to the Atlantic Coast, concentrating the flow of products to New York, aided first by the Erie Canal and later by the New York Central and other railroads."

Neither Astor nor other land buyers could have anticipated that great future for New York and its later astronomical land values. Such people and their heirs are indebted for their riches to New York's visionary Governor DeWitt Clinton, who sponsored the Erie Canal, completed in 1826, and also to fierce capitalists, like Cornelius Vanderbilt, who pushed the New York Central right of way through to Buffalo and later to Chicago.

Chicago became the greatest city in middle America because of its virtually ideal mid-continent port location for handling trade from the Atlantic via the Great Lakes passageway to and from the Mississippi Valley and the West. No other site serves as well. St. Louis is at an excellent gateway spot to the West but lacks Chicago's natural accessibility to the East.

Other U.S. cities were spawned for much the same reasons, because of accessibility to a river and trade routes, turnpikes and railroad lines, though, of course, other reasons can also enter the picture. The site of Ft. Duquesne, where three rivers join, became the city of Pittsburgh, which grew because of its accessibility and because of its proximity to the great sources of coal needed to fuel a giant steel industry in the making. Lancaster, Pennsylvania, was born along the natural route west from Philadelphia, but sprang up at its specific site because of a local water spring. And Syracuse, New York, grew at its site because of the salt mines nearby that gave it its first industry.

Clearly, though, pure and simple accessibility—fast, easy and convenient transportation in and out of an area—emerges as the supreme, most essential requirement to spur the growth of an area. It can happen in an old as well as a new place aborning. When a new international jetport was opened not long ago in Nassau, the Bahama Islands, a land boom erupted and its ripples have been felt up to one hundred miles away.

Other influences on growth

Once a new city has planted its roots other factors influence how it will grow and expand its branches. There is the "follow-the-sun" theory. This holds that many a youthful city, in both new and old world, has expanded to the west and to the northwest because of some unexplainable pull of the overhead sun. It's true that a property on the west side of the street tends to have greater value than on the east because the west side turns its back to the hot afternoon sun in summer. Similarly, and especially before the days of air conditioning, property on the south side of the street also brought a higher price than on the north because the south was cooler in summer. It's just the opposite, of course, in the southern hemisphere.

Many cities expand west and northwest because that is upwind and away from the industrial smoke and fumes of local industry. That was, however, more typical in Europe than in America and especially for many cities in Great Britain and Germany. The prevailing west wind blew the black smoke of soft coal eastward so that upwind to the west was the nicer place to live.

Some cities grew to the west upwind from their cattle stockyards. People in Dodge City, for example, fled westward and upwind to avoid the stockyard aroma and breathe fresh air, points out General Larry Oppenheimer, author of *Land Speculation* and chairman of Oppenheimer Industries, a national ranchland consultant and real estate brokerage firm.

The great appeal of water

A body of water will also exert a major, if not controlling influence on the growth of an area. First, of course, there must be water to live, and virtually no land can be settled today unless water is available. In Colorado, for example, land may be located on the banks of a large, ever-flowing mountain stream but still not have water rights to the stream. Those rights may have been sold or otherwise given in the past to a property owner upstream. As a result, the waterfront land is virtually valueless. And in southern California the growth of Los Angeles and surrounding areas is tied directly to the long, wide aqueduct routes bringing in essential water from the mountains.

The other influence of water has to do with its great appeal to humans. A waterfront site on a river or ocean has the supreme appeal, as anyone who has lived next to water well knows. Thus the growth of Chicago, for example, bucked the more frequent city growth westward. Its growing population streamed northward up the gold coast shoreline of Lake Michigan, pulled by water and waterfront appeal.

New York's choice growth spread east along the north shore of Long Island, Great Gatsby territory, and to the northeast along what is now the yacht-club-studded shoreline of Westchester County and lower Connecticut. Water holds such great appeal that a waterfront property will generally bring a price 50 to 100 percent higher than land nearby that is the same in all ways except no waterfront.

Height combined with water can also be unbeatable, something to remember especially when you shop for country property. The ideal property to look for is one with a panoramic view and a pastoral brook trickling through. Later when you choose to sell the view and the water are guaranteed to turn on city buyers. Water can also increase the value of commercial property, as smart developers know. Nationally admired real estate developer Jim Rouse of Baltimore, for example, has much enhanced downtown sections of his new town of Columbia, Maryland, by putting in manmade lakes.

Turnpikes, railroads, and trolleys

The more typical growth paths of cities followed the routes of the main turnpike or railroad in and out of town. Much valuable property today is along the old original horse routes and carriage lines, which directed early growth almost like a compass. Much basic growth in the Northeast, for example, followed the old Boston Post Road, still called that, which was the route of messengers on horseback in colonial days between New York and Boston to the northeast. Today that same route, U.S. 1, is, in effect, a 200-mile-long Main Street from New York to New England through innumerable smaller cities and towns.

The multiplying railroads, with their valuable right-of-way property across the country, had their impact on growth during the latter half of the nineteenth century. Then came what we can call the trolley car era, lasting roughly from 1900 to 1940 and the start of World War II. New trolley lines fanning out from downtown determined the convenient places for people to live and thus determined land demand. They also spawned little land booms along their lines, as many a smart investor soon realized.

An example is Senator Francis G. Newlands, an admirable liberal member of the U.S. Congress who was also an entrepreneur. Back in 1900 he knew that his bustling little capital city of Washington, D.C., was growing slowly toward its hilly northwest because that was the coolest place to live during Washington's sweltering summers. He sent his agents up Connecticut Avenue to the northwest with orders to buy all the available farms and other land along the way. After that was done he proceeded to build the first trolley line out Connecticut Avenue—and watch the value of all his newly acquired land zoom up.

The heights to which land values were driven up as a result of new trolley and transit lines has been described by Homer Hoyt in this way:

> Land values for retail stores are highest where the greatest number of shoppers are brought to a market and where merchants can make the highest volume of sales per square foot of store area.

Homer Hoyt, one of the foremost land and real estate economists of the twentieth century. In 1974 when this was being written, Dr. Hoyt was 78 and still active.

Prior to the automobile revolution and before 1929, retail sales and land values rose to Mount Everest levels at the converging points of streetcar and elevated lines, as at State and Madison streets in Chicago, or at the meeting points of subway and railroad terminals at 34th Street and Seventh Avenue in Manhattan, and to lesser peaks at highway crossroads on the "Main Street" of smaller cities. Within these districts nearly all the great department stores were located and they were flanked by the array of women's and men's specialty clothing stores, shoe stores, variety stores, and other small specialty shops. From all points of the metropolitan area families came to this central point to shop for fashion goods, which were chiefly articles of apparel.

In those halcyon days of the central retail district, total land values in the Loop of Chicago, less than half a square mile in area, were 40% of the total land value of the 212 square miles of Chicago. In 1903 Richard M. Hurd valued the best retail land in New York City at $18,000 a front foot, and the best retail land in Chicago at $15,000 a front foot, and in Philadelphia at $11,000 a front foot.*

The automobile era

The auto doomed the trolley, but it was the unwinding of the 42,500-mile Interstate Highway System that had the greatest single impact on suburban growth and land values in the United States following World War II. New superhighway links transformed vast areas of former corn fields and sleeping villages into seething suburbs with rapidly mounting land values.

The highways brought growth, to be sure, by making outlying areas speedily accessible to city jobs. Land along local roads and secondary highways feeding in and out of a superhighway interchange soared in value, especially because of demand from the developers of regional shopping centers, and their nearby satellite attractions. The highway boom also fed on itself. As it made vast areas of formerly country acreage accessible, the masses of new housing built created in turn new demand for more stores and services. And so on, round and round, it went.

Besides the Interstate Highway System, other major influences on land values in recent years include the construction of new air-

*Copyright 1968 by the Eno Foundation for Highway Traffic Control, Inc., and reprinted by permission from *Traffic Quarterly* (July 1968).

ports and jetports, large new government complexes like the Houston, Texas, space center, and almost anything large and new that will attract hordes of people, such as Disney World in Florida.

At this point one might conclude that to make a fortune in land, just buy fast at the very first announcement of a major new highway, jetport, or new Disney World, and then you merely sell later at a fat profit, as done in the past when the railroads and trolleys came. It's not quite that easy. For one thing, that's what the crowd does, like lemmings, with the virtually inevitable boom-and-bust cycle and more people are losers than winners.

For another, it can also have its nervous and harrowing moments for buyers, because not every newly announced highway, jetport, or what have you is necessarily built. In 1972 and 1973, for example, many people bought up land and farms around Stewart Airport, near West Point, sixty miles north of New York City. It was in a binge of speculation following news that the airport might be greatly expanded and turned into New York's fourth international jetport. Speculators' prospects of quick profit were, however, sharply dimmed in 1974, when a study by the New York Regional Planning Association concluded that a fourth New York jetport was not really needed. Many investors in land near the proposed jetport suddenly had nervous third thoughts about their holdings. Their nerves were by no means calmed by news that came soon afterward. Because of the energy crisis, the recently expanded Newark Airport to the south, one of the three big New York area jetports, was suffering a drastic loss of airplane business. So why open a fourth jetport?

Even when a major project is built, sending land values soaring, not all the land soars in value. And not all investors do well. Disney World set off a raging land boom in central Florida after it was announced in 1968. Though pushed to high levels, land prices in the vicinity continued to rise after it opened in 1972. But shortly afterward the market softened, and some of the new motels, restaurants, and other businesses there were empty of customers. As a result, prices for the less desirable land still available softened considerably.

The investor who often loses money in land is generally a loser through ignorance, through a lack of understanding of the product bought and how it is used. Often, land is bought hastily, too hastily.

And, of course, some buyers are also done in by a fickle twist of unlucky circumstances, just as others reap a profit by a twist of luck in their favor.

On the other hand, the smart investor who seldom loses with land is generally a winner because, first of all, he knows how to single out land that is most likely to rise in value because it is in a path of

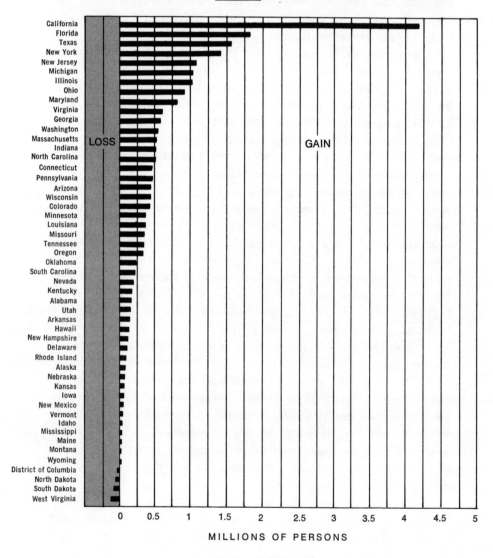

STATES RANKED BY <u>AMOUNT</u> OF POPULATION CHANGE: 1960-1970

approaching growth. He has, in other words, made himself familiar with the kind of growth that is likely to operate within the area. Over the years growth has conformed to a few distinctive patterns that recur time after time.

chapter 4

COMMON GROWTH PATTERNS

The swift growth of the Green River Valley area of Seattle, Washington, shows typical growth patterns, how an area is enveloped by growth and expansion and how land values are pushed up. It also shows and exposes an increasingly dangerous trap facing people who invest in land.

The first signal of its rapid future growth came when a flood control dam was authorized for the upper Green River Valley in 1946. The dam was to eliminate the flooding peril from heavy rains and spring runoffs. For the first time it was apparent that something would be done to make much of the valley habitable and free from the annual flood threat.

But there's many a slip betwixt the cup and the lip. Money was still to be allocated to build the dam; that didn't come until a few years later. People who knew about things bided their time. Then the second growth signal came in 1956, when plans were announced for a new system of freeways for the valley, "thus providing excellent future accessibility to this area," says Michael T. Rancich, a project planner for the Seattle firm of Clark, Coleman and Rupeiks, Inc.

That was the trigger. Land values in the valley zoomed up by 19 percent a year from 1957 to 1959. In the whole decade following that announcement, 1957–1966, they rose by more than 600 percent, according to a study of all land transactions in the area by Rancich.* Quite a few people obviously wanted to get into the game. During that period they bid up the price of land by an average of $787 per acre, per year.

The trap of oversupply

Rancich also found that "although much of the area has been zoned for industrial uses, the estimated future market demand for development will require *a mere 16 percent of the total available land"* (my italics). He concluded, "thus this land will be largely vacant well beyond the year 2020." That's the trap becoming an increasingly large hazard in many parts of the country—plainly more land available than will be needed. Putting it another way, as growth spreads from a central area, increasingly larger amounts of land are brought into the potential market for development, and on an expanding front. A time soon occurs at which the increased supply must surpass the demand.

Often, however, there is a time lag before this fact is recognized, as in the stock market between the time when a trend has reached its peak and a later time when that peak suddenly becomes apparent to people. During the time lag, and before mass recognition, there is a subtle but not necessarily clear-cut change in values. Then everybody seems to catch on all at once, followed, of course, by sharply falling prices.

Not all the land within an area of growth will fall in value, to be sure. The trick is to understand how local growth patterns form and spread, and thereby know which land in an area will be among the small quantity of the chosen 16 percent in demand, or whatever the percentage will be in your area, and how to avoid other land that will go unneeded and unused until sometime after the year 2020, if at all. In the preceding chapter we saw how, first, a city or region is blessed and chosen (or cursed, if you will) by growth. In this chapter we will deal with growth patterns within a city or any other growing area.

*Reported by him in an article, "Land Value Changes in an Area Undergoing Urbanization," in *Land Economics* (February 1970).

Radial growth

Most cities and towns grow in a radial pattern (sometimes called axial growth), or in a concentric circle pattern, or in a combination of the two. Radial growth spreads from the central business district, or CBD, like spokes from a wheel axle. The CBD is the focus of social and civic life. It's usually the downtown point of most convenient access from all parts of the city, and also to and from the main downtown retail district. In smaller cities you'll often find the main banks and offices there intermingled with retail shops. In large cities the financial district often establishes its own separate area, as the Wall Street area of New York and The City in London.

Radial growth streams out from the city center along the main highways or transit lines in and out of town. More than a century of growth in New York City, for example, pushed slowly north along its main artery, Broadway, starting from the original downtown at the Battery. It pushed uptown through Manhattan and the Bronx to the Yonkers city line. Broadway, in fact, followed the natural overland horse route north from the baby village of New York of the time some 160 miles north to Albany, following the east bank of the Hudson River. Virtually all growth along that river-valley corridor was attracted to this right of way, like iron filings to a magnet. Like the Boston Post Road linking New York to Boston on the east, Broadway, or Route 9, became the Main Street of virtually all the riverside towns that were spawned by it on its river-valley route north from New York City.

That's typical, too, for one of the first main paths of growth of any area is from downtown out along the main route to the next large city, and then on to the next one after that. The pattern continues in the form of a chain between two large cities linked together with a series of smaller towns along the way. You can see it in many places, such as Route 41, the main road north from Chicago to Milwaukee, Route 1 from Miami to Ft. Lauderdale and north, and so on.

Trolley and subway lines accelerated the internal growth of New York. Occasionally some transit lines criss-crossed (like the crossing of 12th Street and 4th Street in Greenwich Village is difficult to believe even when you're at that corner looking up at those two unbelievable street signs) and new mesh patterns of growth were spawned. Similarly, Chicago's trolley and transit lines sparked its meshlike growth. The vacant areas within the main radial spokes and fingers of growth emanating from downtown were gradually settled and filled in.

Concentric growth

The concentric pattern of growth, also called the ring pattern, consists of a series of circles forming around the central business district. It's a phenomeon that will vary in shape and depth, of course, according to the city. In general, the first zone around the CBD tends to fill up with wholesale businesses and light manufacturing, the most important support industries required by the CBD. Then generally comes a circle layer of low-income housing for the downtown workers and employees; followed by a circle of houses for the more affluent people; and then the outlying business and residential districts. One authority, E. W. Burgess, sums up the resulting pattern slightly differently in these words:

> 1. The central business district; 2. A transition zone of service industry, trade and commerce; 3. Housing for the working man; 4. A zone of better, higher income houses; and 5. The commuter zone

No city, of course, will necessarily follow the pattern exactly. Besides, both radial and concentric circle forces can be going on simultaneously. Then a "star-shaped" city results, its growth following the main highways or other thoroughfares radiating from downtown, and various degrees of development filling in the areas between.

Sector growth

There's also the sector pattern of growth formulated by Homer Hoyt from studies he did for the Federal Housing Administration in the 1930s. It tends to confirm the circle theory. In a number of U.S. cities Hoyt found that growth from downtown grouped itself into sectors of similar land for similar users. In effect, the sector pattern is birds of a feather flocking together.

All the wholesale food merchants set up their markets in the same area, or city sector. Each draws strength from the presence of others because of their combined use of common sources of supply and distribution. The same is true for the clothing business, the flower district, light and heavy manufacturing, and so on, each in its own sector. A similar pattern is notable today in the development of industrial parks set up in suburban locations to put together a variety of firms with similar needs.

Hoyt found that each sector also tends to reinforce itself, attract more of the same birds, repel interlopers, and by and large push to expand its own sector boundaries. A district of light manufacturing established in an eastern quadrant of a city, for example, will tend to expand its roots, keep others out, not necessarily overtly and sometimes not even knowingly. But like a flock of birds defending its nesting grounds, the members will maintain and reinforce sector solidarity.

Moreover, the members in a particular sector tend to grow together. A high-income residential sector that begins say, in a western sector, will tend to grow and expand in the same direction, and thus generally stay in the same, western quadrant, though the quadrant may increase in size. The high-income people who live there will also, naturally, take over the nicest and most desirable land, as they can pay the most for it. Naturally, that's also likely to be land that is high, dry, and coolest in summer, upwind from smoke and smells, and, today in exclusive suburbia, well away from the roaring trucks and noise of a superhighway or jet airport. The tendency of land use by sector development, like use by similar users, is good to remember when you visit a new growing area where the subtle pattern developing may not be apparent to the casual observer. However, you may notice birds of a feather flocking together within the same block or two or in a particular sector of town, thus the start of a trend. The value of much land there and the prices it goes for in the future is therefore likely to be determined by the same use.

Hop-skip-and-jump growth

By no means, however, does the advancing path of growth sweep up all land in its path. A surprising amount of land is often hopped over or skipped by in a characteristic hop-skip-and-jump manner. This was pointed out to me by Marion Clawson, a leading authority on land, author of many books on the subject, and Director of Land Use and Management for Resources for the Future, a nonprofit research group based in Washington, D.C.

Clawson says, for example, that an owner may hold out for too much money, that a tract may be tied up by an estate problem (with its late owner likely also to have held out too long and too high), or that the next land down the road may be unsuitable for the development desired. For these and other such reasons, much land is commonly skipped over in favor of the next available land sought for the purpose.

The land passed up may remain vacant for a considerable time. It contributes in its weed-grown way to hop-skip-and-jump development and to the surprisingly large inventory of vacant lots and unused land that is found today in most cities and suburban areas. Keep your eyes open and you'll not only see it going naked and unused almost everywhere, but also remember that some of it could be ripe for profitable use now, given the right buyer and user.

Fan-shaped growth

The overall shape that a city or town assumes as it grows out from its center obviously will also be influenced by geography, especially if a river, ocean, or mountain blocks its growth on any side. A developing oceanside area, like many a city on the U.S. Atlantic seaboard, will then fan out in a roughly semicircular shape. If a city is located on a river, a similar growth pattern is likely unless the river is bridgeable. If it is bridged, growth flows over the bridge to the other side, not surprisingly. But the main growth generally will cluster on that side of the river with the principal business and financial center downtown. Kansas City, Missouri, and Kansas City, Kansas, are interesting specimens of the growth of two cities on opposite sides of a river, not only for their past growth, but also for the future growth. The new Kansas City international airport will also have an impact on the area's future growth.

But the fan-shaped growth of an area blocked entirely on one side or another will, by necessity, progress at a different speed and in other different ways from the growth of a city that can spread in all directions. Radial growth contained within the 180 degrees available to a fan-shaped city will occur roughly twice as fast out along each emanating spoke from downtown, compared with the slower speed of growth out from the center of a fully circular city (even though the actual shape is more like a rectangular or square). In other words, growth will march out from downtown about ten miles in a fan-shaped city in the same time that it spreads only five miles out from the center of a circular city.

Use and development of land along the limited semicircle perimeter of a fan-shaped city is thus both more immediate and more valuable than use and development of land along the larger outer perimeter of a circular city. Among other things, land will be needed for more stores and shopping centers on the perimeter of the fan-shaped city because it is twice as far from downtown as that of the more compact circular city. The farther they are from downtown, the less people will want to go downtown to shop. It becomes too much of a fuss and bother. As a result, suburbs naturally develop faster, and farther from downtown, in a fan-shaped city than in a circular city, or a city of any other compact shape.

On the other hand, it also follows that the downtown of a circular city will tend to retain its strength and vigor longer, compared with the fan-shaped city. Again, it's because of logistics. So long as you can get downtown to the old established department stores, and restaurants as well as amenities like the theater and concert hall, they will flourish. (Of course, matters of public safety and crime can adversely affect downtown areas.) The key is that such downtown attractions must remain sufficiently accessible to enough people to maintain themselves—in other words, downtown clearly must continue to attract enough people to stay in business.

The fan-shaped city, however, offers more promise for investing in land because its semicircular perimeter is swelling faster with growth. More stores and other businesses open there to serve the growing number of people who turn away from downtown; that's where the great need for land comes from. Obviously, it comes sooner in the fan-shaped city.

New growth in an old area

In 1960, the planning department of Westchester County, New York, issued a report predicting widespread new growth throughout the county in the decade to come. Westchester is a commuter's county, home for many of New York City's high-income executives and businessmen. One reason for its predicted high growth rate was the

construction of new highways, some planned, some nearly completed at the time, to facilitate traffic in and around the county's large
land area. One of them at the time was the new Cross-Westchester
Expressway, a wide, six-lane superhighway spanning the twelve-mile
lower waist of Westchester, from the Connecticut Turnpike on the
east to the New York State Thruway on the west. It was the final
interstate highway link for traffic between New England on the one
side and the tier of mid-Atlantic states, including New Jersey and
Pennsylvania, on the other.

The impact of the new expressway was felt not long after that
report came out, and it shook up everybody's predictions. At the
time, the forward thrust of Westchester County's growth had long
since passed beyond the center of the county, the area traversed by
the new superhighway. Nonetheless, this road suddenly, by itself,
became the single major attraction for much of the county's ensuing
growth. New businesses and industries sprang up along its east-west
corridor like mushrooms after rain. In fact, more than half of all new
growth and development in the county during the 1960s was concentrated along the Cross-Westchester Expressway corridor spanning the lower middle of the county, according to John Levy, Director of Research of Westchester County's planning department.

Levy told me that the new expressway was "the most significant
influence on land use in the area in the past twenty-five years." Land
values soared all along its corridor route. One of the last available
large properties near it, a 100-acre site zoned for low-density office
use, was sold in 1973 to a national corporation, Pepsico, for a reported
$10 million, or $100,000 an acre. That's an unusually high price for
land restricted to relatively low-density use, Levy said, with much of
the tract to be given over to lawns, trees, and wooded areas. The
unfolding path of a new superhighway not only will open up development of a rural area but, plainly, can also stir a resurgence of growth
in a mature suburban area where the growth front has already passed
through. (Of course, it can also cut an asphalt swath through wooded
country and quiet residential areas, as in Westchester, alas, where it
cut up and wiped out much splendid country land and clusters of
houses on lovely landscape.)

Caution on future highways

Not every new highway that may be proposed or planned will necessarily be built and completed in the future. So don't rush out and buy a lot of land along any and every predicted new right of way. Even along those that *are* built, as some bond holders will sadly tell you, spectacular growth doesn't always follow. It is wise, therefore, to be cautious in considering land investment along a new superhighway. It is not always a sure thing.

For one thing, the highway lobby, including politicians, bureaucrats, and make-work engineers, sometimes makes mistakes in determining the need for a new highway, or in choosing the best location. For example, the wide asphalt swath of still another superhighway in Westchester County, Interstate 684, was extended north from the much-traveled Cross-Westchester Expressway a few years after the expressway was completed. But the new highway is, by comparison, hardly used. It is still not complete at the time of this writing, to be sure. But still many a person who bought land along its right-of-way corridor may have to wait a while before growth catches up and makes his land more valuable.

For another thing, the energy crisis has, so far, cut down on superhighway travel. One result is reduced toll income and in some cases deficit operation of some superhighways. That's not exactly happy news for officials who sponsor new highways and, more important perhaps, for investors who buy the bonds to finance them. They are understandably cautious about proposals for the construction of any expensive new highway. We can expect that the need for each new highway will be subject in the future to more probing examination than in the past.

To sum up: a good new highway can indeed spark much growth in and around the area it travels. But no one should assume that growth will automatically follow. And therefore no one can invest in land along its route with guaranteed assurance that the land will rise in value.

Other growth influences

New growth in an area also can be sparked by almost any other development that is a magnet for people. It may be a new government center, an institutional or corporate complex, or just a big new factory. The growth of the upper Green River Valley area outside Seattle got a shot in the arm in 1966, for example, when the Boeing Corporation announced plans for three large new plants there. That rejuvenated the land boom because as many as 50,000 new jobs would be created. It takes little imagination to visualize all the land required for the housing, stores, and other needs that inevitably follow such an influx of people.

Rural growth in a resort area or any other country place is also directly related to its accessibility to the outer world, however wondrous its rural appeal. This was pointed up in a little-known study by Richard Irwin of the U.S. Bureau of the Census covering the years from 1960 to 1970. He found that the presence of a good major highway, or "freeway," made a remarkable difference in the growth of small towns and country areas. His conclusions were based on his study of 102 counties in various parts of the United States, the largest city of each ranging in size in 1960 from 7,500 to no more than 50,000 people. In nearly every case, the counties with a freeway for access and egress grew in population at a rate "two to three times faster" than similar counties with no freeway.

The exceptions in Irwin's study were a few small counties in which, despite the lack of a freeway, growth was spurred by the presence of a college, military installation, or "public institution." In the future, to be sure, a college will have less influence on growth because our college-age youth are no longer swelling in numbers as they did during the last decade. There is also a lesson in Irwin's study for anyone who tends to be carried away by advertisements for glamorous resort property or retirement homes or charming country property. Don't buy unless there is a good wide highway nearby, if only for your own convenience. That is, unless, of course, you want to be alone like Garbo, or seek to commune with nature like Thoreau.

General rules of growth

Two tendencies are common in most city growth:

1. Each layer of society tends, like water, to seek its own level according to income, common survival needs, and social position. It's a kind of automatic social or commercial segregation that also operates, by the way, in other behavior. (Among other things, it is a

natural social force that must be acknowledged and understood before true racial integration can ever be achieved.) Naturally, the richest people will seek the best, most expensive land for their homes, the next highest income group obtain the next most expensive land, and so on along the scale.

2. The principal growth generally appears on the periphery of a developed area, its fringe. Seldom in the past have people turned back to downtown and given rebirth to an old area. Older sections are generally rebuilt to a new use. This natural tendency, however, has been fought by government planners, to be sure, who have sunk huge amounts of money into mishandled attempts to modernize older areas under the guise of urban renewal. A notable exception is the rebirth of the West Village in downtown New York, discussed with firsthand knowledge (because she lived there) by Jane Jacobs in her book *The Death and Life of Great American Cities.*

From these two basic growth tendencies are derived the following general rules, including some points mentioned earlier:

• High-income residential growth tends to move from its point of origin along a main thoroughfare out toward the next nearest concentration of high-use property.

• People in the richest, most fashionable areas tend to move toward high ground and hills or in the direction of the nearest water. That's assuming no landblock or drawback dead ahead like a mountain or noxious industry. This historic trend to the hills is evident in many cities in America, particularly so in a celebrity area like Beverly Hills, California. The inexorable attraction of water is shown not only by New York and Chicago, but in other areas with a large body of appealing water nearby: San Francisco, Boston, and Palm Beach.

• Zones of high-priced residential houses also tend to be attracted toward open country beyond the city's periphery. They are repelled by a dead-end location where expansion is limited by a natural or artificial barrier.

• The houses belonging to community leaders and prominent people—the rich and the celebrated—tend to form a growth nucleus, attracting new residential growth around them.

• High-priced residential areas are often located near the main office buildings, banks, and stores in town. This is, of course, because the businessman, the bank president and store owner choose to live close to their work to reduce commuting. So you often find high-income housing established close to the central business district.

•   High-priced housing areas tend to be located along the most direct and convenient access to the city.

•   The growth of a high-income residential area, once begun, will continue to move and grow in the same direction for many years.

In sum, the growth of nearly all areas follows a pattern. You can see this by becoming familiar with your own town, how it grew and how it continues to grow. Go over a map of the expanding perimeter and notice the barriers as well as the highways, and other influences that are shaping and influencing its growth. Notice the kind of land that has been chosen for the most expensive houses, the luxury expensive stores, and the highest value commercial development. Why is each located where it is? What about the main highway or other thoroughfare leading from your downtown to the next largest community? Make a few of your own predictions about the path that future growth will take. Which land along the way seems likely to become highly desirable, if not essential, for future growth? Once this is determined, and you have decided you would like to buy the land, your next decision is when to buy, which brings us to the matter of good timing, the second fundamental requirement for successfully buying and selling land.

chapter 5

THE CRUCIAL IMPORTANCE OF TIMING

The best time to buy and sell land, of course, is when you can buy low and sell high, as the old cliché goes. Most people who do that, however, had it planned all the way.

Consider, for example, some smart young men I know with IDC Real Estate, a national firm with headquarters in Chicago. Off and on they got requests about buying land from various people. Somebody would call or drop in the office and say, in effect, "Have money, want land to invest in. Know any good acreage for sale?"

Finally, the IDC men said, "Okay, let's do something for all these guys. We'll go out and find some land to invest in and arrange for these guys to buy it. We might even buy a few shares ourselves."

They did exactly that, and within a few months after buying the land it had risen in value by 50 percent. Here's how it happened, as described to me by Gary Waterman, executive vice president of IDC Real Estate.

The original investment goal was for land that would double in price in three to five years. Where was the best place to look for it?

We singled out the planned Elgin-O'Hare Expressway as a future growth corridor. It was a new highway coming through that would almost certainly raise land values all along the route. But then, exactly which land there would be best to buy? And what was available?

We had one of our men research the corridor for six weeks, its whole length west of Chicago and north of O'Hare Airport. Besides finding good land at a good site, what about its price, the terrain, and obviously such things as the zoning and future use potential?

By elimination we zeroed in on a twenty-acre farm that was available. Then came the practical considerations. Could you build on it? What about the utilities, water, drainage, and especially the sewer situation?

Then, naturally, we did market research. Who could use it later and add up to a good buyer? And, most important, what would it be worth to him in a few years when we would be ready to sell?

Well, we bought the land for $10,000 an acre, its market value at the time. A few months later we turned down an offer of $15,000 an acre for it. We felt that properly developed and marketed, it will be worth $40,000 an acre in a few years when the expressway is under construction and everybody can see it's happening.

The timing of that land purchase was almost ideal, occurring just about the moment at which the value of the land was beginning to rise sharply. Such timing is important because, contrary to popular thought, the value of land just does not rise steadily and inexorably over a long period of time.

The three stages of land values

The life cycle of land generally falls into a three-stage pattern, as illustrated in simplified form in Figure 1, devised by Stephen Roulac, president of Questor Associates, a Menlo Park, California, consulting firm, and a lecturer at the University of California, Berkeley.

In the first, or undeveloped, stage, the land generally lies fallow or is farmed for a long time. Its value rises little from year to year, though its dollar price might climb because of dollar inflation. The first stirrings of imminent development marks the end of the undeveloped stage, and things change.

Enter the second, or predevelopment, stage. It could be signaled by news of a proposed new highway, a new bridge, an airport, or any other development that means land action and that things will be jumping soon. That's when a real estate man gets excited, his pulse speeds up and his imagination soars with dreams of financial glory, and not without good reason. The value of land begins to climb

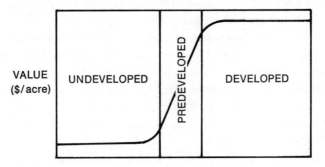

steeply during the predevelopment stage, which generally lasts about five or six years, more or less. During this stage the value of land can rise as much as 20 to 30 percent a year, sometimes more, before leveling off, in other words, doubling in value in two to three years, and then doubling again fast.

The cost of improvements

Not all of that price rise, however, is necessarily gravy for the owner. A portion of it will come from the installation of water, sewer, and utility lines and other improvements that, of course, represent money invested in the land. This is important to remember because some people, lusting for future profits, tend to overvalue raw land during this stage based on its value as improved land. Yet little or no improvement has been done and little or no value has been allowed for it. Moreover, the cost of improvements can mount up to as much as 50 percent of the ultimate value of developed land, possibly more. So ignoring this hunk of cost can be particularly costly for a buyer. The rise in the value of land levels off when it is ripe for development and ready for use, which marks the start of the third and last stage of the cycle. Now its value is determined, naturally, by its use and its income from that use.

    Ideally, you would neatly step in and buy a hunk of land, on cue, precisely at the beginning of its predevelopment stage, in other words, just before its value is propelled steeply upward. Then later, since you're batting 1,000, you would ideally sell just after its value has peaked and has begun to level off. That, however, is the dream world. In real life, nobody, including the most astute professional, ever bats 1,000, or even close to it. But by knowing that such a thing as ideal timing points do exist, and certain cues often signal it, a reasonably smart investor—amateur or professional—can achieve reasonably good timing. The main difference between the amateur and the professional, of course, is that the professional does it more often, which hones his skill. Any newcomer to land need not be cowed, however, by his lack of experience. It can be overcome by working with a good professional when buying land, as described in chapter 10.

And knowing that there is a best time to buy, or sell, if only roughly when that time may occur, can help even the rankest amateur avoid or at least minimize two highly common mistakes. The first is buying land too early in its particular stage; the second is waiting too long and buying land after its rising value has little upward momentum.

The high cost of holding land

Buying too early can be an expensive mistake because holding land can cost you about 10 percent a year of its price. That's long been the rule-of-thumb cost you pay for annual property taxes, liability insurance, and such things as the finance charges on money borrowed to buy. There's also the loss of return from the same capital otherwise invested elsewhere, or just resting in an interest-bearing bank account.

That 10-percent-a-year holding cost for land should be revised upward as interest rates and money costs rise. In 1973 and 1974, for example, the prime rate for top bank loans rose to over 12 percent, and home mortgage loans climbed to over 10 percent (assuming you could get one). Then it was said that land values had to rise by 16 percent a year just for the professional investor to break even because of the high price he had paid for borrowed money, according to the editors of *The Real Estate Review*, the professional journal.

Besides, money put in vacant land, sleeping peacefully for years, could be tied up peacefully for years, like Rip Van Winkle, because of the illiquidity of land as an investment. Clearly, the earlier you buy in advance of the predevelopment stage, the higher your holding costs and the lower your ultimate profit (assuming there will be a profit).

Still another trap awaits you should you buy good land but decide to sell too early, even if you've got a live buyer at a good price and potential tidy profit for yourself. You may be at a stage where you can practically smell your profit, but don't start spending it. For selling land before it is ready for development generally will mean that the buyer will be another investor or speculator, and not one who will develop and use the land. Few banks or other lenders will, however, put up the money to finance vacant land except when it's ready for development. So you, the buyer, generally must finance the seller.

Financing a land purchase or sale

Consider a 150-acre farm in upper New York State that was bought by an investor a few years ago for $12,000. Its value went up fast, at least on paper, and not long afterward he was offered $21,000 for the place. Fine, except that the best terms he could get from the buyer were $6,000 down payment in cash and the balance ($15,000) to be repaid in fifteen years, with annual mortgage note installments at 7½ percent interest a year. Not only will the seller have to wait a while for his profit, but he's stuck at a lower-than-average interest rate that soon became obsolete.

The down payment for land that is financed is generally no more than 29 percent of the sales price so that the seller can spread out the income tax payments due on his profit. A larger down payment ordinarily makes the seller obligated to pay the full tax due on any profit in the same year as the sale. Actually, the Internal Revenue Service says that the cutoff point for that tax liability is 30 percent, the top down payment that will allow a seller to space out his tax on a profit. The figure of 29 percent is the limit customarily used in the real estate business, apparently to be on the safe side.

So don't start counting your chickens when you discover a seemingly unbeatable bargain in land that you can't afford to pass up. Buy too early in its undeveloped stage, and the cost of holding it over the years could wipe out the future profit. Sell prematurely, even at a hefty paper profit, and it could be years before you have that profit as cash in hand.

The high profit of good timing

Buying land at the beginning of its predeveloped stage will pay off with the highest and handsomest profit when you buy it with a low cash down payment. Put up little capital, in other words, and take advantage of maximum leverage. That's according to a study carried out by C. Wesley Poulson, president of Coldwell Banker, a national real estate firm.*

This study shows that the highest profit comes when land is bought with a cash down payment of only 5 percent, maximum leverage, and then sold within five years after purchase. Then you can earn from 30 to as much as 50 percent a year net on your money invested! That's based on a climb in the value of the land of 20 to 25 percent a year, or a doubling in the value of the land in less than four years. The higher your income tax bracket, the higher the net profit. As shown on pages 62–65, the yield comes to 29.9 percent for a person in the 30-percent income tax bracket, up to 50 percent in the 50-percent tax bracket.

Poulson says, however, "In reality land with the greatest appreciation potential cannot always be bought with a small down payment, for the owner of property in the path of growth can demand more cash down." But even then your profit is nothing to sneeze at. It can be a net after-tax yield ranging from 15 up to 33.5 percent a year with a down payment of 15 percent, the study shows. Again, the higher the tax bracket, the higher the net profit.

Those figures are based on 7.5 percent interest charged on the money financed to buy the land, the typical rate levied when the study was made. Should that low rate be unobtainable, a remarkably high yield is still possible with a low down payment and the balance financed at the next best interest rate. That's also based on selling the land within five years.

The profit on land held for ten years can fall off considerably. It will range from a high of 22.75 percent a year with everything going for you, to less than 1 percent. Buying land that you must keep for more than ten years is generally a losing proposition, with some

*"Using the After-Tax Discounted Yield to Compare Investment Alternatives," available for $2 from Coldwell Banker, 533 Fremont, Los Angeles, CA. 90017. After-tax discounted yield, or ATDY, is the annual rate of return after taxes on the outstanding balance of the original investment at the end of each year.

exceptions, to be sure. A braggart may crow about all the money he made in land over a long period of time but he's usually blind to his true net profit. It's usually small, if not nonexistant, after taking into account all his long-term holding costs (for taxes, etc.), not to mention the greater sum he probably would have earned had the same capital been invested elsewhere, or simply kept in the bank over the same period. The main exception would be a long-shot bet on very low-cost land, assuming that, like John C. Lincoln, you bought at the right place at the right—very, very low—price. But most people don't live that long.

Poulson makes two other good points. He says that making a profitable investment is also a constant battle against:

1. Overpaying for the property—not only in relationship to other similar properties, but also in comparison to after-tax yields on other investment opportunities. This is the most critical error, for if an investor overpays for the property he cannot operate it efficiently nor resell it favorably.

2. Acquiring a property which does not meet . . . [your] investment objectives—the tax planning takes place after the property is acquired rather than before.

To sum up: the importance of good timing when you buy land is inescapable. It boils down to judging the transition point at which land passes from its undeveloped to its predevelopment stage. In the long history of most land, that's when it enters its one and only major growth phase, and that's when it begins its one and only steep rise upward in value. One of the few exceptions, to be sure, is when a change in zoning suddenly puts a sharply higher—or lower—value on land.

Very few people, however, can expect to achieve ideal timing simply because the precise moment at which land can be bought for maximum future profit is just plain too hard to predict, especially without hindsight. Or, among other things, the land is unavailable at the time. Nonetheless, that transition point from one stage to another does occur and merely knowing about it and coming reasonably close to it can be highly rewarding.

As a matter of fact, it generally is better to wait a while and buy a little late, rather than a little early. Waiting to be sure that the time has come for a particular tract of land may cause you to pay a somewhat higher price, compared with buying earlier. But the odds are much greater in your favor that the time *has* come for the land to appreciate. Buying too early leaves the door wide open to the risk of buying prematurely, and then you could be a long time waiting for things to develop.

Another way to beat the game, conventional wisdom has it, is to benefit from secret advance knowledge about a planned new highway or other such development. Obtaining such inside knowledge can be a help to be sure, though sometimes it can also be a false alarm. It is also by no means essential. The best-laid plans of politicians, as well as mice and men, often go astray. There is almost always time after such news is made public to appraise its impact on the surrounding area, and still buy good land at a low price, and profit well later.

The three best times to buy land

There are, in fact, three best times to buy land. The first is at the very beginning of the predevelopment stage when its value begins to climb upward. That's when the first news is heard that something is going to happen. It's when a new highway, bridge, or what have you is initially announced. Land prices in the area will rise overnight, but if the event is later confirmed and realized, values will later rise even more.

The second time is the day before the projected new development is confirmed with reasonable certainty. This could be when the money for a new highway is appropriated and no major roadblocks lie in its path. Or when the contracts for a large new industrial complex or shopping center are given out. No general definition can be given to describe when this next best buying time occurs because the kind of confirmation can vary according to the event. Of course, a few people will know this time the day before it happens, but for the smart investor its significance will sink in fairly soon after it happens. At this time land prices will have reached a plateau following the sharp rise after news of the development (the first buying signal) became known. Now after the confirmation occurs—and this may take a year or two, if not longer, after the first news came out —land values start climbing again and then level off at a second, higher plateau.

The third best time is at the spade digging—when construction actually starts. Then land values take off upward for the third and last time. Very little question remains about the development not going through, thus the least risk associated with an investment in good land at a good location nearby. Still many people won't believe it until they actually see the work happening, and many others not until they see the work actually completed. That's when the final holdouts are convinced and when land values hit their highest level.

The total time elapsed from the first signal to buy land until later when a major growth development has run its course through its predeveloped stage can last from about five years, more or less, to as long as ten years, sometimes more. Again, it depends on the circumstances. Growth lasted close to a decade in Rockland County, New York, where I live. Much good land was available there *after* the news came out, following World War II, that the New York State Thruway was coming through, and also *after* the Tappan Zee Bridge, the last link of the Thruway between upstate and downstate, was completed across the Hudson River and its first toll gates opened for business in 1955. Rockland subsequently was one of the very fastest-growing counties in all of New York during the following decade.

Similarly, excellent land investments were still to be made by astute investors on the west side of the Mississippi River across from New Orleans after the river was bridged there and after the planned West Bank Expressway there became a certainty and sparked a fortune-making land boom. Many other such examples could be cited, including the Dallas–Ft. Worth airport, which provided opportunity for investors well after it became public news. As described in the next chapter, that example also shows that you may have to pay a higher price than otherwise for good land, but that can be chalked up as the insurance-premium extra cost one pays for more certainty and less risk.

The above should put the importance of good timing in perspective. We must also stress that all land in a particular area does not necessarily and suddenly undergo a rapid and sudden phase of change, from its first into its second stage of development, at the news of a major happening in one part of the general area. The ripples spreading out may not reach out to all the land that will be affected for some time. There is not just one "best" time to buy, however; there are three.

In sum, good timing does not necessarily require instantaneous action, like all runners being off at the crack of the gun. It does help, however, if one applies to it some judicious knowledge and thought and then acts within a prescribed period of time.

ANNUAL AFTER-TAX DISCOUNTED YIELD ON LAND INVESTMENT

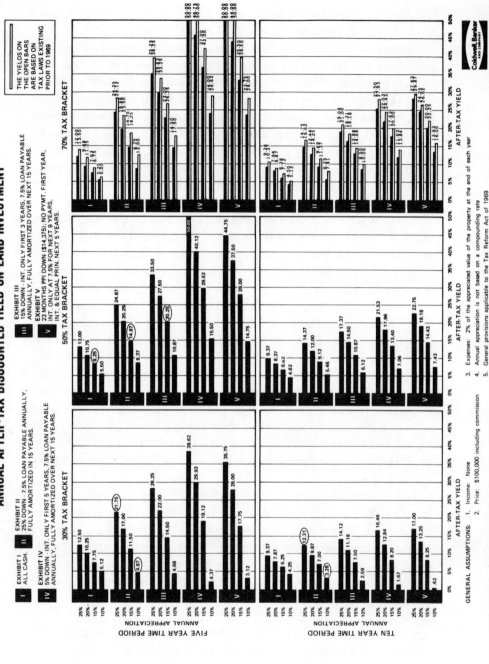

Coldwell, Banker AND COMPANY

NOTES

The land investment chart gives the investor some idea of the general range of yields he can expect in a land investment, given different terms and appreciation factors as well as holding periods.

The after-tax discounted yield on a land investment is the product of three components:

(1) Terms on which land is acquired (amount of down payment and the payment schedule on the interest and principal portions as well as the time allowed to pay back the debt).
(2) The period of time the property is held.
(3) The amount of appreciation received over the holding period.

Once the investor has acquired the property, and the terms of the sale are made final his yield is the result of the period of time he holds the property and the amount of appreciation that occurs.

LAND INVESTMENT GUIDELINES

Effects of Borrowing

When considering a purchase of vacant land for speculation, the investor should attempt to negotiate terms which will give him the highest after-tax discounted yield with the least amount of annual appreciation. For example, the terms in are 25% down, a 75% note amortized in 15 years. If the property appreciates 15% annually and the property is sold at the end of the fifth year, the return to an investor in the 50% tax bracket would be 14.87% (refer to the figures which are circled on the chart). This is compared to an "all cash" return of 8.25%.

If the property can be acquired with only a 15% cash down payment, the return to a 50% taxpayer at the end of 5 years would be 20.25%. Although the Land Investment chart illustrates that an investor can generate a much larger yield with a smaller down payment, in reality properties that have the greatest appreciation potential cannot usually be acquired with small down payments, for the owner of level property in the path of growth can demand a greater down payment. The best land buys in an area are generally a compromise between terms and appreciation potential.

Effects of Income Tax Rates

Land investments have more appeal for investors in higher income tax brackets because the carrying charges are deductible, and the tax on the profit is limited by the capital gain provisions.

Optimum Time to Sell

The longer the property is held, the less effect terms have on the yield. For example, by acquiring a property under the terms of Exhibit II, a 30% taxpayer would have a yield of 21.75% with 25% annual appreciation, and a 4.87% yield with 10% appreciation annually. Therefore, at the end of 5 years the yield spread would be 16.88% (21.75%–4.87%). Refer to the figures circled on the chart. The same yield spread on a 10-year hold is 9.03% (12.31%–3.28%). If the property were held 15 years, the range would be narrower, and in the 20 to 25 year range the yield range would almost be non-existent.

The optimum time to sell land to maximize the yield is within the first 5 years of ownership. Once the property is held beyond this time period, value must increase 25%–30% yearly in order to give the investor the same rate of return as that received if the property appreciated only 15% yearly during the first 5 years of the holding period. Since quick appreciation is a vital element in making land speculation profitable, properly timing the acquisition and resale is critical.

Supporting Expense Data for Land Chart

25% Annual Appreciation FMV	5-Year Hold Year	Expenses	10-Year Hold Year	Expenses
100,000	1	2,000	6	4,500
125,000	2	2,500	7	5,000
150,000	3	3,000	8	5,500
175,000	4	3,500	9	6,000
200,000	5	4,000	10	6,500
225,000 Resale				350,000 Resale
20% Annual Appreciation				
100,000	1	2,000	6	4,000
120,000	2	2,400	7	4,400
140,000	3	2,800	8	4,800
160,000	4	3,200	9	5,200
180,000	5	3,600	10	5,600
200,000 Resale				300,000 Resale

15% Annual
Appreciation

100,000	1	2,000	6	3,500
115,000	2	2,300	7	3,800
130,000	3	2,600	8	4,100
145,000	4	2,900	9	4,400
160,000	5	3,200	10	4,700
175,000 Resale				250,000 Resale

10% Annual
Appreciation

100,000	1	2,000	6	3,000
110,000	2	2,200	7	3,200
120,000	3	2,400	8	3,400
130,000	4	2,600	9	3,600
140,000	5	2,800	10	3,800
150,000 Resale				200,000 Resale

chapter 6

HIGHEST AND
BEST USE

A well-known American athlete, a superstar with super earnings during his career, used to put a good portion of those earnings into buying land when he was riding high. He bought land almost anywhere, all over, as an annuity for the years after he would retire. He could not lose, he figured.

Only now, after retirement, he has found to his grief that much of the land he bought is unsalable, except at distress prices. In many cases it is worth no more and even less than what he paid for it ten to twenty years ago. Someday demand may build up for his land holdings and make them valuable. But he may need patience.

He made "one of the biggest and most common mistakes I continually see made with land," says Bill Howard, a land specialist vice president with the Los Angeles office of Coldwell Banker, the real estate firm. It's a mistake made by people "who buy land with no idea whatever of its future use," Howard says.

In short, not only is good timing important, but before buying land you should determine what the land will be good for later. And most important, what is its best use? That's the third most important phase of investing in land, after its location in relation to future local growth and good timing.

Value according to use

Real estate people use the term "highest and best use." It tells you, in effect, whether land will be worth a few thousand dollars an acre or $50,000 to $100,000 an acre, if not more. Basically, land is valued according to its "ground rent," or the income from its use. Land being used as a site for two three one-family houses an acre might have a capitalized worth of, say $10,000 an acre, depending on location and the sales price of the houses. Used for ten to fifteen apartments per acre, it could jump sharply in value. Again its exact price depends on the location and the apartment rental income. It works the same way, of course, with land used for commercial, industrial, or any other use: the income from the use determines the price of the land.

Densities and Number of People Per Acre for Various Housing

Type of units	Average density per acre	Average number of persons per unit	Total average number of people per acre
High-rise	67.73	3.3	223.5
Medium-rise	45.00	3.3	148.5
Garden	19.55	3.4	66.5
Townhouse	13.62	3.5	47.7
Single-family	2.50	3.6	9.0

Land for multi-family housing increases in value according to the housing density, but not necessarily proportionately. For example, land for high-rise apartments had an average value of $175,000 an acre versus land for single-family houses at $15,458, according to 1969 study that is source of above figures. Averages value of the land also varied from $1,711 to $2,582 per family for the four densest housing types, compared with $6,183 per family for land for single-family houses. *(National Association of Home Builders.)*

Highest and best use is defined by the American Institute of Real Estate Appraisers as "that use that at the time of appraisal is more likely to produce the greatest net return to the land and/or building over a given period of time." The Urban Land Institute calls it the use "that will produce either the highest present land value or the highest net return."

Five main categories of land value

The highest use will naturally put the greatest value on land. In general, land falls into the following five main categories of use and subsequent value:

1. *Commercial:* office buildings, stores, shopping centers, hotels, motels, restaurants, and so on. The high income from these will enable the owner to outbid all other users for the land he wants. He can outbid others, obviously, because his income on the land will generally exceed the income from any other use at the site.

2. *Industrial:* a factory, industrial park, warehouse, truck depot, or other manufacturing facility.

3. *Residential:* mainly single-family and low-rise housing. In recent years, however, the price of housing has risen so sharply that land for higher-priced multi-housing, most notably luxury apartments and high-rise condominiums, sometimes will pull it into a category of higher use, making it as valuable as land for a high office building, which is the most expensive land of all.

4. *Recreational or resort:* parks, camp grounds, marinas, ski trails, and so on. In recent years recreation and resort areas have proliferated but now have a questionable future because of the energy crunch.

5. *Agricultural:* farm and ranchland. Whether or not such land is actively farmed or grazed, it is statistically counted as farmland by U.S. Department of Agriculture economists, one of the chief sources of land price figures.

Determining the value of land

Most users can tell pretty quickly the top price they can afford to pay for land. A shopping-center operator can often figure out on the back of an envelope how large a store he can put up on a certain site. The sales volume he can expect from that size store can then be quickly estimated, leading him to the maximum price of land that such sales will support.

A home builder is likely to use the current rule of thumb that says his land cost should not exceed 25 percent of the sales price of the houses he can build on the land and sell in the local market. He may figure that he can sell houses on a site at up to $80,000 apiece. Assume that the zoning permits one house an acre. His land cost,

Average Price of Finished Lots; Ten Highest and Lowest States in 1969

State	Average price
1. Hawaii	$15,791
2. New Jersey	10,920
3. Connecticut	10,313
4. California	9,507
5. Washington, D.C.	9,267
6. Delaware	8,875
7. New York	7,958
8. Illinois	7,569
9. Massachusetts	7,197
10.Ohio	6,922
State	Average price
1. Wyoming	$3,000
2. Idaho	3,200
3. Kansas	3,709
4. New Mexico	3,998
5. South Carolina	4,034
6. Tennessee	4,099
7. North Dakota	4,455
8. Arizona	4,431
9. Indiana	4,718
10.Texas	4,746

These average land values are mainly for suburban land outside of metropolitan centers except for the lowest valued land much of which is in or near small cities and towns. The cost of improvements (spent for water, sewer lines, streets, sidewalks, etc.) represents more than 50 to as much as 75 percent of the average prices shown. By 1975, the same land had, by and large, climbed in value by another 60 percent approximately. *(National Association of Home Builders.)*

therefore, cannot exceed $20,000 an acre (25 percent of $80,000), including what he must spend for improvements (roads, water, sewer lines, excavation, etc.), in addition to the price paid for the raw land. If his improvements will cost an estimated $10,000 an acre, that leaves him no more than $10,000 an acre to spend for raw land.

Suppose he's dickering for land with Jack Hufflewhite, a local property owner with acreage for sale. Like other owners of land, Hufflewhite is not necessarily familiar with the builder's cost profile, and he wants the very highest price possible for his lovely acreage. He asks $16,000 an acre, but the builder demurs. Hufflewhite comes down a step or two but then issues an ultimatum: "I'll take $12,000 an acre but not a penny less."

The builder refigures his costs, including his development costs. He reviews the results of the market survey to determine whether higher-priced houses might be salable there, but decides not. He concludes that he was right the first time: $80,000 houses are the top limit for this land. He tells Hufflewhite that $10,000 is the maximum he can pay for the land, and then he heads down the road for the next best land available at a price he can afford to pay.

If, however, the local zoning were suddenly changed to permit two houses an acre, then the land would nearly double in value, and Hufflewhite would be sitting pretty. If water or sewer lines, or both, were already there, the land would become even more valuable, because the price to improve it would be lower. Land, by the way, formerly accounted for about 12 percent of the sales price of new houses, it reached the 25 percent rule-of-thumb level only in recent years. If land prices keep rising faster than construction costs, that 25 percent rule of thumb could climb even higher in the future.

Much the same kind of figuring and negotiating goes on when commercial and industrial users seek land, though the stakes are higher. Little or no guesswork is involved; some professional land speculators may think otherwise, but they should know better.

Not long ago, for instance, a Georgia real estate broker and investor in land, Joe Magnum (not his real name), paid $5,000 an acre for land near his home town, some fifty miles northeast of Atlanta. It was at a future interchange site for Interstate Highway 85, then under construction from Virginia to Alabama. Like other people in the business, he knew that his land could become a prized commercial site. It could bring a high-dollar price from an oil company, in particular, for a high-volume gasoline station.

Sure enough, within six months an oil-company agent came by and offered him $80,000 for a choice corner section of his land. Joe held out for $90,000—and ended up with nothing. It was indeed a good gas-station site, but not at Joe's inflated figure. The oil company man said, "No thank you," and went down the road and bought land at the next interchange. No one else would pay Joe's price and he was stuck with the land. Joe told me later that he learned a lesson. "I profited from my mistake, and I've since made other successful land deals."

Understandably, location more than anything else determines a site's highest and best use, and subsequently the price it will bring. But not everyone can buy a choice interchange corner, or a prime corner site on Main Street, or any other obviously desirable location, especially early in the game. Determining a valuable future site has its fine points and is not always as easy as it may seem later with hindsight.

Evaluating land

Consider, for example, the high stakes played for by professional investors in Texas who were not sure whether to buy land at the north or south entrance to the huge new Dallas–Ft. Worth International Airport, the world's largest jetport. It was hard to say which would ultimately prove to be the more valuable location for future hotels, motels, and other high-priced development. During the airport's construction in 1970–1973, some buyers spent about $50 million for land at the north entrance, while others spent about the same sum betting that the south-entrance location would prove to be better.

The airport plans were proposed in 1965 and large tracts of land in the vicinity, midway between Dallas and Ft. Worth in north Texas, immediately jumped in value to $1,000 an acre. "That was a substantial increase over previous prices for land there," a local real estate man says. Much of the "first-seller" property was bought at that price level, from original owners, largely farmers and ranchers, though development of the airport was by no means certain at the time. Some original owners held on and saw their land increase in value up to the neighborhood of $3,000 an acre during the next three to four years.

The second phase of the land cycle came in 1970 when the airport became a virtual certainty, and land prices there spurted up again. "Then the airport boundaries were established and corporate investors knew what they were buying," says Bill Thompson of the Wm. G. Thompson Investments, Inc., a large real estate investor in Dallas. Miller had been following the airport plans closely from the sidelines but did not jump in and start buying land till then.

Thompson and his group bought some 1,200 acres of land in the next three years. He bought at the *north* entrance to the airport and spent a reported $30 million for land there. He says, "We paid above market value at the time just to be able to get the land . . . but despite the high prices paid, we made some incredible buys." During that time prices climbed up to $8,000 to $10,000 an acre by 1971 and leveled off at that plateau for a while. Construction of the airport speeded up in the next two years. In the fall of 1973, just prior to the airport's opening, land in the vicnity with good road frontage was going for $30,000 an acre, Thompson says, large tracts with no front-age for $16,000 an acre.

Thompson and his group chose to put their money on the north entrance to the airport because it's serviced by the Lyndon B. John-son Freeway, Interstate 635. He told a reporter, "I can prove to you that 90 percent of the travelers will come from Dallas, and 75 per-cent of the Dallas users will come from North Dallas. People from North Dallas, Richardson, Highland Park, and University Park will use the LBJ Freeway because it's closer. With all those passengers, percentage-wise, the hotels and other such places will go up there first," Thompson said. He backed up his opinion with more than a few dollars. He also believes that he has another thing going for his choice of the north entrance, its topography. It's on good dry land. On the other hand, he says the southern entrance is on low land, "subject to flooding from the Trinity River, and there's no plan for road improvement at the southern gate."

Other big investors obviously think differently and bet on the south entrance. It could be a little while, however, before it becomes clear which airport entrance, the north one or the south one, exerts its dominance as the favored route in and out of the airport.*

Thompson also believes that despite the airport being largely completed, it is still creating excellent opportunities for land invest-ments in the area and will continue to do so for some time. In some cases "you may have to pay a great deal for land, but it will be well worth it," he says.

A pattern emerges that often occurs. There is the land that

---

*Just before this book went to press Thompson told me that all signs so far indicated that land at the north entrance was indeed winning the north-south land sweepstakes at the airport, though the final score was still not in.

often becomes available from skittish investors and owners who begin to back out of their long-term holdings and sell prematurely. Buying land even in the immediate area also should be profitable, he says, though it may take ten years. Eventually, he says "there will be a whole new downtown area at the airport, like the Galleria ten miles from downtown Houston."

There is also the spreading ripple effect that has pushed up land prices as far as forty miles away from the airport. According to Robert Wegner, Director of Land Planning for the North Central Texas Council of Governments, values have shot up chiefly within a twelve-mile radius embracing the Denton, Dallas, Ft. Worth triangle. It's formed by Interstate Highway 35, which runs south from Oklahoma and splits into two separate highways at Denton, I–35E to Dallas and I–35W to Ft. Worth. Thompson believes that the ripples will extend forty miles out from the airport for good land along a good highway.

Buying on the right side of the street

Merely buying any good highway land that you think will have high future value by itself may not be enough. Fine points about it can make a difference; one side of the highway may offer greater promise than the other for highest and best use.

Albert Gobar, a southern California land economist and national market research expert says, for example, that "for most businesses, being on the 'going-home' side of the street for people leaving a recreation area, tourist attraction, or large shopping center is a real plus for sales."

But, ironically, it doesn't always increase the value of the land on that side of the street. It doesn't, Gobar says, because some businessmen who buy sites for new stores and other business locations aren't always as smart as they should be. They will sometimes buy across the street, the poor location, because the land is cheaper there. As a result their companies will suffer ever after; their sales will always be lower than those of businesses located on the going-home side of the street. A lesson here is that it may be incumbent on the owner and seller of land on the better side of the street (you) to prove why his land there is better and worth more.

Avoiding the landlocked site

Just as a good road can make a whole area accessible and therefore make land along the route valuable, accessibility to each site along the road is also crucial. Yet a surprisingly large quantity of land misses out on its highest use because of inadequate or no road frontage. Because it's landlocked, it goes for a low price. Such sites are often snapped up by naive buyers who are influenced more by the low purchase price, seemingly a bargain, than by the high cost, if not impossibility, of providing good access to it.

Land with no road frontage near the new Dallas–Ft. Worth airport was as noted earlier, selling for almost 50 percent less than comparable land nearby with good frontage for a good reason. The difference represents the estimated cost to put in a new entrance road and whatever else is needed to make the land accessible. Some-times, though, a landlocked site may require considerably more than bulldozer treatment and an entrance road. An easement from an adjoining land owner may be needed, and that can cost you dearly, assuming that it's available at all. Other traps may lie below the surface. However low the price, such land should be approached with the caution ordinarily reserved for entering a jungle.

Topography

Three other major influences over the highest use possible for land are its topography, the availability of utilities, and, of course, how it's zoned. The first step in checking topography is by personal inspec-tion. Only a fool buys land without seeing it, walking its boundaries, and picking up some here and there to feel, smell, and examine. (That's no different from the same advice given for seeing and check-ing anything before buying. The American Express people, among others, learned this to their multimillion dollar horror when they accepted tons of salad oil a few years ago sight unseen.) Checks by a few experts also may be recommended, such as test borings and a porosity test (for determining sewage disposal).

The drainage characteristics also should be checked. The drain-age pattern of a whole area, as well as that of an individual large site, often can be gauged from aerial photographs, and best of all by firsthand view from the air. Bill Kingsford, a young real estate broker with the IDC real estate people in Chicago, flies his own plane regularly over developing Chicago suburbs to spot what he can't see from the ground. This includes observing flood patterns, "especially after a heavy rain," he says, and also "new growth patterns developing which you can see well at rush-hour time." Two common topographical drawbacks to avoid are low-lying land subject to flooding and steep hilly land that will turn off a developer faster than a nest of rattlesnakes.

Utilities

The availability of water, power, and sewage disposal has always been important, but the latter two have grown increasingly critical in recent years. Gas energy is no longer available for new construction in many areas where formerly it was practically given away, and switching to all-electric building can mean highly expensive operation. Lack of sewer lines has killed more than a few opportunities for high land use.

Checking on utilities obviously should be mandatory before land is bought. But don't necessarily turn your back on land if obtaining one or the other is said to be a tough nut to crack. A little ingenuity or special knowledge might solve a seemingly unsolvable problem. As described later, a bright real estate man I know converted a marginal property into high-value land by buying a small adjacent lot that permitted access to a sewer line that was otherwise unreachable. And new ideas, like the new aerobic sewage-disposal unit (described in chapter 11) sometimes can turn the trick where septic tank disposal is not permitted, and thereby make a lot usable where formerly it was not.

Zoning

Zoning controls have long been the cause of civil war in city and suburb, since they exert iron-clad control over how land may be used. But merely obtaining the current zoning classification from the town hall may not be enough. Will local officials issue a building permit? Sometimes no, even though your proposed building conforms to the zoning. How flexible, or rigid, are the officials who enforce the zoning? Often a more liberal zoning ruling will be issued simply on request; other times the officials will not be swayed by a Mack truck.

And then, of course, there is potential opposition to a proposed use by a horde of environmentalists, who may or may not have a good case. Life is getting more complicated than ever, and such controls over land use go right up there near the top of all the complicated matters that can arise, unless you happen to live in one of the few areas with no zoning, such as Houston, Texas. There may, however, be a silver lining to a cloud of such complications: although they may be tougher to overcome, he who does overcome them can expect much greater rewards than ever before.

chapter 7

THE IMPACT
OF THE ENERGY CRISIS

It hit like a sledgehammer in the bleak winter of 1974. Long lines of cars queued up at gas stations, and their drivers nervously wondered if there would be any gas left by the time they reached the pumps. Those long lines of cars, dramatically shown from the air and seen on television, showed us just how much our society depends on energy and just how vulnerable we are without it. In this case, the energy crisis came when a handful of Arab oil sheiks decided to turn off some spigots.

Its impact on land was swiftly felt when the flow of guests to hotels, motels, and restaurants that depended on motor travel fell off sharply. Business was sharply off for snow resorts in the North and sun resorts in the South. In Florida a real estate expert told me that at the height of the January 1974 gas crunch, many motels and restaurants in the area of Disney World in central Florida, ordinarily filled close to capacity, were like ghost towns.

Throughout the country, real estate brokers reported that practically no one came out to shop for new houses. It was as if a broad, no-energy moat suddenly sprang up between every metropolitan area and the open country beyond. Hardly anyone passed through it. Among the hardest hit were those with country property for sale.

Later, of course, gasoline began flowing again, though its price shot up by more than 50 percent. (At the same time fuel oil for houses and industrial uses doubled in price in many areas.) Within a few years, increased worldwide supplies of oil and gas, plus expanded supplies from other energy sources, plus for the first time, major efforts to reduce waste, should temper the impact of possible future energy shortages. Nevertheless, things will never be the same again.

For one thing, many a person will think twice before deciding to settle out in the country and buy some property. For another, mass transit systems for cities have suddenly achieved a practical acceptability, especially in the U.S. Congress, where formerly the highway lobby and power brokers like Robert Moses decided how the bulk of our transportation billions would be spent.

Energy impact on land

How will all of that affect the future value of land?

Almost certainly the value of much country land and land out along the open road will suffer at least partly. That's not necessarily because of diminished need for motels, restaurants, and gas stations serving travelers and tourists. But many people who influence such land use will understandably *think* in terms of diminished demand for such uses, and therefore cause diminished demand and purchase of that land.

Here are other ways in which the energy crisis is likely to have its impact on land, according to a review of experts' opinions I made for this chapter.

• Land for new housing and ancillary needs will climb most sharply in value in areas closest to the nearest jobs, in other words, to the nearest thriving business and industry. "Closest" doesn't necessarily mean as the crow flies. Quickness and convenience in time of travel between the two places is the key requirement. Thus the best locations will be those with easy highway accessibility, or good public transportation for quick travel to and from job centers.

The value of such land will climb even higher in the future than in the past because more higher-density housing will be built in the future. We should also remember that more smaller, compact housing will be needed in the future, not only because of the growing number of families with fewer children than before, but also because of the growing number of couples with no children and single people living alone.

• More new towns, like Columbia, Maryland, and Reston, Virginia, probably will be built. In the future they will be located close to mass transit lines to reduce automobile travel. The new towns so located will probably be among the few new developments that will put a premium large tracts of vacant land out in the country.

• Central ghetto areas "will not benefit from the flow back to the central city unless whole sections are renovated or cleared, and the crime rate reduced," predicts Homer Hoyt. He also says:

• "There will be an increase in demand and value for farmland yielding income." That means timber, mineral, and grazing land, as well as regular crop-bearing farmland.

In all, the energy-crisis decade of the 1970s coupled with environmental restrictions will drive up the value of well-located, desirable land. That means land that can be built on now. It will drive down the value of other land that is poorly located and land that cannot be built on for ecological or other reasons. The result will be a vast difference in the value of vacant land in any area, city, suburb, or suburban fringe, depending on its accessibility and, to put it in the ultimate terms, whether or not a building permit will be issued for its use.

How mass transit makes land valuable

In February 1970 teams of workers began digging up the streets of downtown Washington, D.C., as construction began for a new, long-overdue mass transit subway system that will fan out to the suburbs on all sides of the city. The first thirty-five-mile section of the system is scheduled to be completed and opened for service in late 1975, and another five years or so will be required to complete the rest of the new mass transit system for the Washington area.

But very few people seeing that digging underway every day since in Washington, and walking and riding over plank-covered holes in the ground, have more than a rudimentary idea of the impact of that new system, not just on travel and commuting in and out of Washington, but also on land values spreading out for about 50 miles in nearly every direction from the center of the city. That embraces a total land area, by the way, of close to 8,000 square miles and more than five million acres of land. Well over 75 percent was vacant and unused land in 1970 when the new subway system was begun.

Other new mass transit systems are being considered or planned in a growing number of other cities. Plans are already drawn for them in such cities as Atlanta, Baltimore, St.Louis, Jacksonville, Buffalo, and Pittsburgh, according to Cody Pfanstiehl, operating director of Washington D.C.'s Metro system. If in other cities future transit is not largely by new high-speed aluminum trains, it could take the form of high-speed express bus lines being put into service, especially for rapid travel within smaller metropolitan areas in less populated parts of the country.

A new transit-line's impact on an area's growth and development will be much like it was in the past. In the previous chapters we saw how the old trolley systems and subway lines influenced the expansion path of mushrooming cities like New York and Chicago in the nineteenth and early twentieth centuries. Outward growth from downtown followed a new trolley or train route, like an arrow, almost as if programmed into each transit line route. Hustling real estate men and land brokers followed the announcement of the new train and trolley routes much as they followed new highway plans in recent years.

The station stops were the nuclei of new growth in the past, just as later superhighway interchanges created new growth centers along a superhighway corridor. In the words of Richard Hurd back in 1904, the new elevated-train stations located, one after the other, up the west-side spine of Manhattan in New York City, at 72nd Street, 81st Street, 93rd Street and 104th Street, and so on, were "starting points for new territories in which growth took place in all directions." (Station locations are not all the same today because of subsequent changes in the New York City transit system.)

The corner sites at each station stop became the most valuable land. Each successive parcel down the block away from the station had somewhat diminishing value. That's plainly because each corner site is accessible to all the people pouring out of the station, but each store down each block going away from the station is accessible to only one-fourth the number of people pouring out of the station after a train has arrived.

Future mass transit systems fanning out from a city into the country, however, will very likely have a more diffusive impact on people traffic and greater leveling effect on land values near each station. That's because now in the automobile era people can range farther out from each station to more distant home locations. In the past the homes of most people were, by necessity, within walking distance of the station.

Another example of the concentrated growth that often followed, especially at four-way transit intersections, has been described by Homer Hoyt in his classic book *One Hundred Years of Land Values in Chicago*. The streetcar caused a shopping-center boom in Chicago from 1915 to 1929: "at streetcar intersections in the city, five to seven miles from the downtown center ... each [intersection area] contained branches of department stores, variety stores, specialty apparel stores, banks and movie theaters." Hoyt wrote that the "aggregate land values of these satellite loops skyrocketed from 1910 to 1929. . . . The values of sixteen of the best shopping-center corners increased ten times [during that period] from an average of $435 to $4,313 *a front foot!*" Those, of course, are pre-Depression, pre-inflation dollars. They would be equivalent in 1975 dollars to some $10,000 a front foot. The 1929 crash wiped out that era, to be sure. Like nearly everything else, land values collapsed.

Mass transit case history: BART

Still another future effect will be sharply increased price tags for land located at the downtown city stations where new transit lines unload masses of people from the suburbs. This was dramatically shown by a study of the impact on property values in the San Francisco–Oakland area by the new Bay Area Rapid Transit System, BART. The study, carried out by researchers at the University of California, Berkeley, showed that the most significant impact was indeed on property values in downtown San Francisco and Oakland at BART's inner-city terminal stations. City land values rose sharply, particularly in the downtown areas south of Market Street and adjacent to the BART route in San Francisco.

Speculators perked up their ears, naturally, when BART's initial plans were first announced in 1956. But land values in the area did not begin to rise much until 1962, when its route and station locations were made public. The real land action, however, began only after construction of BART started in 1968, and people began to believe that the new transit system was for real. Then land along its route in downtown San Francisco rose, "on the average, more than 100 percent" in the next few years, according to the University of California report.

BART was a major influence on the downtown land boom at such sites, according to the report, because of the new real estate spawned there. At least eleven skyscrapers were planned for the sites, including new offices for Standard Oil of California and the Wells Fargo Bank. Top company executives chose such locations for their new headquarters largely because of the favorable logistics. BART would provide convenient commuting for new employees from a broad outlying region. That could assure each company a large pool of people to draw on for employees, particularly for executive talent. Downtown stores and other businesses would also benefit, naturally, from the large numbers of commuters pouring in and out of town.

Impact on suburban land

Not surprisingly, the study also found that land values also perked up along much of the three main BART lines fanning out from downtown San Francisco and Oakland. The biggest impact, of course, hit at the site of the BART's thirty-three station stops. The greatest increase in land and property values was for land "immediately adjacent to the BART stations, first for commercial property, followed by land for apartments, retail establishments and then for one-family houses." The most desirable sites skyrocketed in value. In 1973, a Contra Costa, California, realtor said, for example, "I listed a little piece of property, about an acre and three quarters, for $63,000 ten years ago. Two years ago I sold it for $575,000. Now that same property has a ten-story building on it and is probably worth three-quarters of a million dollars."

Not all of the land along the 71 miles of BART lines rose in value, however. For one thing, much of BART runs down the middle of automobile freeways. For another, quite a few speculators were carried away in the initial BART buying spree from 1963 to 1966, when the first bond appropriation was passed to build the system. They bought too far from station stops or too far out beyond the end of the line. According to the authors of the Berkeley report, such buyers bought land at "tenuous locations . . . and are [still] waiting till the market catches up." Clearly, their timing was poor. They bought land too early in its undeveloped stage. That common mistake made here also emphasizes again the folly of getting caught up by crowd psychology and buying any land, anywhere, in the first flush of an exciting new development.

Some speculators along BART's three main routes will also be "bitterly disappointed" because of rough new environmental rules over land, according to Anthony Dehaesus, a Bay Area public plan

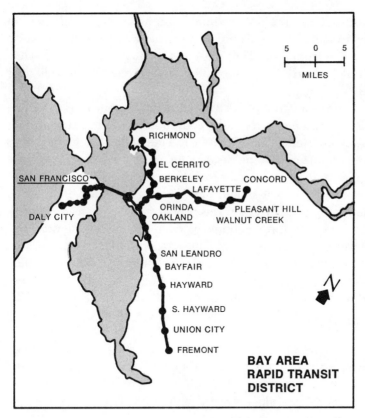

BAY AREA
RAPID TRANSIT
DISTRICT

Not unexpectedly, land values rose the most at the station locations along the route of BART's mass transit station. They rose highest of all at the downtown stations in San Francisco and Oakland.

ner. In certain places, he says, local government officials are cracking down hard on new development plans, closing loopholes in the zoning laws and simply being hard-nosed about every proposed new kind of building and land development brought before them. As a result, he says, "A lot of heavy speculation in these areas will not be realized."

In sum, the new Bay Area Rapid Transit system has clearly been a major spur to business, commerce, and industry, to virtually everyone, and to society as a whole in central California. It has, naturally, opened large land areas for new growth and development. That's in addition to its giving a new lease on life to land along its route in downtown San Francisco and Oakland. Such a major new growth catalyst introduced in a region should not, however, be taken as an invitation to speculate anywhere, in any way, with a surefire promise of getting rich from land. That's not just because you must be selective, but also clearly because of new environmental controls over land use.

Now the launching of BART's pioneering train runs (mostly a no-hands' operation controlled by computers) has not been without its snags and problems. These include the inevitable mechanical bugs that have arisen, plus some serious financial operating problems. These apparently arose because top operating management was not as financially astute as it should have been. Among other things, a derailment of one of BART's trains brought down a cascade of criticism of its new operating technology, even though no one was hurt. Soon afterward an old-fashioned Chicago commuter train, operated by live humans in overalls, derailed with a bloody crash that killed or seriously injured, in all, some thirty-five passengers. Yet there followed no press or public uproar of the kind that followed BART's little mishap, which by comparison, was no more than a dented fender.

New kinds of mass rapid transit systems have by no means been discredited, and they are highly likely to multiply throughout the country. As each one is born it should have a major impact on local land and real estate values—and properly planned, a major therapeutic impact on a whole region.

A typical growth sequence

A new mass transit system like BART will trigger a series of events conforming to a pattern, according to Lee Syracuse, a California planner and market research consultant with a special interest in the social implications of growth. Syracuse may have a downbeat view and some people may disagree with his ideas, but the pattern he sees can help put the influence of a new transit system into its long-term perspective. His step-by-step pattern of events goes like this:

a) Realtors will buy up small parcels around stations in middle-class residential areas.
b) Local governmental response will always lag behind development pressures, with court action sometimes necessary to bring about change toward higher densities.
c) The time required to achieve moderate density (22-25 units per acre) will be about two to three years. The developments will be just beyond walking distance to the stations. Thus, assuming that feeder service will not be provided, in BART's region, autos will be used for access.
d) Within ten or fifteen years, the traffic generated by a BART-like station will be overwhelming to the neighborhood.
e) This is the time when big investments will make themselves felt in the area. Pressure will be placed on the planning commission to make large changes in zoning and parking regulations, height limitations, etc. Various experts will be brought in to offer testimony in favor of highway density, and the community will be put on the defensive of having to prove that the present zoning is "realistic." Eventually the city will accept development.

Syracuse's last two points could be open to argument as the last great land boom runs its course. That will be as it dawns on a growing number of people that there is considerably more land available way out there than many people think. This should become increasingly clear as new rapid transit lines open up many large areas of outlying land that may be far greater in size than even the biggest, the most insatiable demand appetite for land can digest.

chapter 8

HOW TO SHOP
FOR LAND

Take a little old corner plot of land that nobody wants, add some imagination, a missing ingredient or two, and then let simmer for a while. Then presto—you could turn a handsome profit in a surprisingly short time!

That's how it happened for a smart real estate investor I know who was willing to take a chance. He bought a corner plot of land not far from my home not long ago for $100,000. He tidied up the place and put $30,000 more into making it salable. Some thirteen months later he sold it for $220,000, a profit of $90,000 in less time than it takes an elephant to be born.

The land Don Carter (not his real name) bought was a corner plot of 1.82 acres on a major north-south highway, New York State Route 303, in Orangeburg, New York. It's some twenty-five miles northwest of midtown Manhattan. I had driven past it often and noticed the "For Sale" sign on it. The sign had been on a tree there for nearly two years with no takers. Anyone interested, the sign said, could obtain more information by calling New York's Chase Manhattan Bank.

The land is located in a bustling area zoned for commercial and industrial use, so getting permission for commercial or industrial use was no problem. Yet still no takers. Along came Carter who also lives and works in the area. The land bothered him. It was too good a site to go unused for so long. It had an excellent location in a growing, thriving area. He figured that its time had come, and he would do something with the land. Together with a business acquaintance, he bought the land for $25,000 down in cash, and a $75,000 note to finance the balance.

Then Carter went to work. Part of the problem with the land was the difficulty of providing sewage disposal for it. He proceeded to buy a small adjacent piece of land, .68 acre in size, because that would provide a route for the installation of a sewer-line feeder from his corner plot to a city sewer line that was otherwise unreachable. That additional land cost plus the cost of installing the feeder sewer line came to $30,000.

Then Carter did some facelifting. He had the site cleared of brush and weeds, had a bulldozer smooth out its appearance. "The place looked a mess before," he told me. The plot was no longer unattractive. Actually, he says, "The new sewer line made the major difference, but it sure didn't hurt to clean up the plot and have it look good, too."

"Then we put it up for resale," he adds. "We took a calculated gamble, of course. But I felt that it was too good a site to go very long without a buyer. There was no activity for nearly a year, and then a store developer came by and bought it." Carter and his partner speculated and won. Not one person in a thousand would have even considered such a speculation, much less put their money behind their conviction.

Carter's little coup also points up a parenthetical lesson for those cynics and single-minded social critics who scream condemnation at every speculator in the real estate business who turns a profit (naughty word). Here was fallow land that was doing no one any good and that no one wanted. It wasn't even an attractive part of the environment. Minimal property taxes were paid for it each year to the town, county, and state. It was nothing, in fact, but a blighted eyesore until speculator Carter came along and made things happen, with positive results for everyone concerned.

The public treasuries (local, state, and federal) were enriched to the tune of thousands of dollars of capital gains and other taxes paid by the seller on the price received from Carter for the property, plus the tax money paid by Carter and his partner on their profit.

New jobs were created. Besides the labor to develop the property and build on it, permanent jobs will be provided for x number of people in the businesses established on the property after it is developed.

Local consumers will get a break in two ways. Convenient new stores will provide easier and quicker shopping for many people in the area. And, the new stores will increase competition in the area, which usually means a better deal for consumers.

Now, that's not to say that blessed are all real estate speculators, and that they are the hope of the world. There are, to be sure, some villainous speculators who are outright charlatans and crooks, just as there are charlatans and crooks in and out of government and in the arts and the professions. But just as reasonable men acting reasonably can rid government of a charlatan, so can charlatans be disposed of without killing off a whole of business to rid one organ of a cancer. The free lance entrepreneur, more than anyone else, has, in fact throughout history accounted for most giant strides made by man. Beethoven's Fifth Symphony wasn't written by a committee. Penicillin wasn't discovered by a conglomerate, and utopia has yet to be achieved for us by any big brother government agency.

Buy locally

Now that this author has gotten that little sermon off his chest, there's also a very practical lesson illustrated by Carter's successful speculation. His coup dramatizes the rich lode of ore that can exist right in your own area. In short, buy locally. It's trite, but true; there could be acres of diamonds to be mined in your own back yard. It's no more trite, though, than carrying bags of money to the bank.

Look for land locally, says Alvin Arnold, editor of *The Real Estate Review,* because you can be most familiar with local patterns of growth and local trends, especially in politics and planning. And you're there all the time, right on top of things when important things may happen, even though an important happening may rate no more than a casual comment at a cocktail party, or a few lines in the back of the paper. You can, in other words, stay abreast of what is happening in your own back yard better than you can anywhere else, including a distant place where you might think the grass is greener.

The same advice also applies for you who want to buy country property. Stick to a country area that you like and know. By and large, that means an area you are familiar with as a result of spending vacations there. That doesn't necessarily mean, of course, hands off any area that you are unfamiliar with. But once you choose to shop and buy in an area that catches your fancy, then it behooves you to get to know it well and become familiar with it.

Let's suppose now that you've decided to buy some land. You will seek a good investment in the area where you live. Or possibly in a country area where you have a vacation house or where you would like to vacation or retire.

What's your next step? What's the best way to find good land for sale? Answer: *Work with a good local broker.*

Of course you will read the real estate ads for land for sale. As you drive around, also keep an eye out for land with a "For Sale" sign on it. Driving down country roads and into remote areas is part of every professional's shopping plan.

But not every owner who decides to sell land instantly nails up a "For Sale" sign on a tree in front, and not every owner calls in an ad to the local paper. Many an owner, in fact, has a personal aversion to such public announcements. Many owners merely pick up the phone and list their land for sale with a broker or two. What's more, much of the best land of all is continually sold through brokers, with nary a bit of public advertising or promotion.

In a booming area, as a matter of fact, just finding good land for sale is no easy task. Nearly everyone knows, for example, that in recent years the land business has been booming in Arizona and that it's likely to continue to boom there for another decade or two, according to the economic indicators that signify such behavior. The buying and selling of land goes on there, day to day, in such a seething seller's market that just finding someone with a good slice of land to sell is an achievement, according to Rob Ward, a land specialist in the Phoenix, Arizona, office of Coldwell Banker.

In 1973, Ward told me that each of his land brokers once a month makes it his business to call on every owner of land in his territory. What's the latest status of the man's land? By any chance has he considered selling his land in the past month?

That can be called keeping on top of your market, as well as staying ahead of your competitors. That's also how a good broker wins friends and influences people. When an owner of desirable property finally decides to sell his land, naturally he'll think of that nice young man who has stopped by so often. "The man who always asks about my health, and says I've got such a great place here. If I ever wish to sell he says I could get top dollar for it. Well, that's the man I'll call now and say that I've decided to sell."

The broker gets the call from old Jake Potter saying that Jake thinks he just might consider selling his land now. Now things get hot. But by no means does the broker instantly nail up a "For Sale" sign on the property, or prepare a newspaper ad about it.

Instead, the broker pulls open a desk drawer and leafs through his select list of clients who are prime customers for land. He goes down the list, balancing off each one's desires, his price require-ments, and credentials, one after the other, against the requirements for buying Jake's land.

In short, to buy good land in a hot market, you may have to get in line early and wait your turn. Not always, to be sure. But no matter where you start shopping for land, part of the shopping should in-clude a mandatory tour of the best brokers in the area. Seek out those who specialize in land, including those who, off and on, will put together land investment packages for buyers.

To become familiar with the local brokers in the area, notice which ones place the most advertisements for land in the paper, as opposed to advertisements for houses. But also remember that ad-vertised land is not always the best land to buy. It may be perfectly good land but overpriced, or it's simply not ranked sufficiently high in value to be picked up by a smart buyer on the broker's master list of clients.

Ask around for the names of the best brokers who specialize in land. Ask the head of the local real estate board, a banker or two, a few appraisers. Also see the people who deal with real estate taxes and records at your town hall or county courthouse. Nearly everyone will mention his own favorite broker, but press on for the names of two or three others. One or two names will predominate. You'll hear them mentioned continually, and then you will have a line on the leading brokers in the area. But don't see only them. Also see others.

The *Realtor** broker

There are some 900,000 licensed real estate brokers in the United States. Anyone may become one simply by working in the business a little while—the minimum term varies according to the state—and then passing a state real estate examination, which isn't noted for being particularly tough. People who get licenses to deal in real estate include taxi drivers, housewives, insurance salesmen, plus many others who desire to make a little extra money moonlighting in their spare time. Because of the on-and-off nature of the real estate business, it is difficult, if not impossible, for most licensed brokers to make a living working fulltime at it.

A minority of all licensed brokers—less than 150,000—are also realtors. A realtor is a licensed broker who is also a member of the local real estate board and a member of the National Association of Realtors (formerly called the National Association of Real Estate Boards). The realtor, by and large, is the cream of the crop. He'll let you know this by a "Realtor" sign in his window and a note on his business card saying that he is a "Realtor." On the whole, the realtor is in the business fulltime, though many a realtor also may sell insurance or do related work, such as being a real estate appraiser, too.

Realtors are generally, though not always, more professional than run-of-the-mill licensed brokers. Every realtor is pledged to conform to the realtors' *Code of Ethics,* which is a good thing. Occasionally, though, a realtor has been known to slip in his adherence to the code. But when one does mention the code of ethics, get a copy of it from him. Keep it for reference.

Summed up, deal with a good real estate broker. As a rule, dealing with one who is also a realtor can mean extra points for you. However, don't necessarily chalk off a broker who is not a realtor. There are some very good, if not excellent, nonrealtor brokers, particularly in sparsely populated and country areas where there are fewer realtors than in the suburbs and cities. A good nonrealtor broker could serve you every bit as well as many a realtor.

Incidentally, when you buy land through any broker, realtor or nonrealtor, the broker's fee, or commission, is customarily paid by the seller, just as the broker's fee for selling a house is paid by the

*Realtor is the registered trademark of the National Association of Realtors.

seller, not the buyer. The broker's fee on a land sale is customarily 10 percent of the sales price of the land. The customary broker's fee on a house in most urban areas is 6 percent, up to 10 percent for selling houses and farms, as well as land, in many small towns and rural areas.

There is no reason, therefore, to hesitate calling on real estate brokers when you shop for land because of the fear that dealing with them will cost extra money. Even more than houses, land for sale is listed with brokers. The larger the tract, the more likely it is to be listed with and sold by a broker.

Land sold without a broker

Of course, land is also sold by many a seller with no broker in the middle to slice off 10 percent of the price for his fee. Then the seller, naturally, will pay no sales commission to a broker. It's his fond wish, of course, to sell for the full price with no sales fee dished out to a broker.

You, on the other hand, might have good reason to bargain for part or all of the broker's fee, getting it in the form of the purchase price being reduced that percentage. Your success will depend on the particular circumstances and the bargaining power you can exert on the seller.

If the seller has also listed the land with a broker or two, he was therefore prepared to pay a broker's fee if it sold that way. That gives you good basis for requesting that at least a portion of the broker's fee be deducted from the sales price. Besides, a broker could have helped you, you can justifiably maintain. Without a broker you can maintain that you provided some of the broker's functions ordinarily provided to the buyer, as well as to the seller. A broker could have simplified the deal for you, but no broker involved required all do-it-yourself effort by you.

On still another hand, the seller may have stepped in and served as his own broker, paying for advertisements, and other expenses, and expending his time and effort for things that a broker otherwise would have supplied.

By serving as his own broker, the seller can thus equally maintain that he was the broker, in effect. Therefore he deserves to be paid the broker's fee. What eventually happens plainly hinges on how the land transaction is handled and sold without a broker, and also on the negotiating muscle that each of you can bring to bear in your favor. You're playing for stakes equal to as much as 10 percent of the sales price of the land, which is nothing to sneeze at. Therefore the ingredients that go into influencing who gets part or all of that pot are also nothing to sneeze at.

Get in the swim of things

Besides getting to know brokers and keeping in touch with them, like any good doctor or Indian chief, you will also want to stay abreast of happenings in the business. Subscribe to a trade journal or two—check on which ones are for you in a good library. Subscribe to a trade newsletter or two.

Also stay abreast of the latest land transactions: who bought and sold which land, the original asking price, and the final sales price paid. Visit such land and see for yourself why one piece of land may have brought a higher—or lower—price than another one that may be similar.

Keep in touch not only with knowledgeable brokers, but also with the clerks and other hands who run things at the courthouse and in the tax assessor's office. They not only know a lot about current real estate dealings because of the papers that pass through their hands daily, but they also pick up much other information simply by being told it by the stream of lawyers, brokers, and others coming in to transact business with them every day. Such scattered bits added continually to your information bank can be invaluable some day as pieces fit and form pictures.

Not everyone, of course, may have the time to check such things and stay in close touch with happenings in all the ways I have just suggested. Actually, top professional brokers and investors do it all the time, or they have hired hands to do it for them. Over the years they also have narrowed down their surveillance, like a good intelligence agency, to those few sources who have proven to be the best listening posts. That, of course, is the trick in every business. But if you're also dealing with a good broker or two, checking in with him off and on can serve much the same purpose.

Fact versus rumor

That calls for filtering out fact from rumor. Even a piece of news from someone considered to be a highly reliable informant still must be checked and verified. Consider, for example, the case of Bob Foster-macher, who came into a family windfall and decided to invest it in land. He lived in a growing area, and at his monthly lodge meetings he had heard how people he knew had made killings in land, or so they boasted. Bob visited a few real estate brokers and looked over the land listings they showed him. He mulled over a couple that struck him as good buys and drove out to see them.

A large tract at the south end of town appealed especially to him because it was a lot of land for a low price. He drove out again after a rain storm to be sure it wasn't flooded with water; it wasn't, and he bought it.

He also bought another parcel in a distant suburb because a business acquaintance told him that a big downtown department store was going to launch a shopping center there. He paid a high price for this land. But, after all, he figured, a new shopping center in the area nearby could triple his money in a few years.

Five years later Bob took stock of his holdings. The land on the south side of town was now surrounded by a blighted area, and he couldn't give it away. He had got it at a bargain price because he caught it on the downtrend. The other land parcel he had bought did indeed rise in value, but not nearly so much as expected. The proposed shopping center he had been told about wasn't very accurate hearsay. It was in fact built—twenty miles to the northwest of Bob's land. His land nonetheless rose in value because, out of the blue, a new highway was built a few miles away. He was therefore able to sell this parcel shortly afterward at twice the price he paid. That worked out to a gross annual profit on the price he paid for the land of 13 percent a year compounded for the five and a half years he owned it. But after deducting his ownership costs (annual property taxes, insurance, legal fees, etc.), his net profit came to 6 percent a year compounded. That's not counting his other, unsuccessful, purchase, which, of course, put his total investment in land in the red.

Yet a very little time and effort spent on the telephone before he bought his two parcels of land would have told Bob that he was diving into treacherous waters. A phone call direct to the main office of that department store would have informed him that, yes, the store was planning to build a major branch in a new suburban shopping center being planned. That was no longer a secret. At the time, the store had also narrowed down the choice of location of the center, as soon to be announced in its annual report, to two main sites. Contrary to rumor, neither one was near the land Bob planned to buy. Such information was not printed in the local paper but was still easily obtainable.

To check on the wisdom of buying all that other land so cheap at the south end of town, a few calls would have disclosed that economic storm clouds were gathering over that part of town. The county planning commission was concerned about it. Calls to a few banks, including his own bank, would have disclosed that local lenders were backing off on giving mortgage commitments in that area. That, by the way, is an indicator of area's decline—a drying up of bank mortgage money in the area.

That brings up the importance of research before investing in land.

chapter 9

GETTING THE FACTS ABOUT LAND

Let's say, for example, that you pick up the morning paper and lo and behold, a front-page story breaks the news that a new bridge will be built across the local river. It will open up the whole other side for miles to new development that people have been predicting for years. But shucks, the average reader thinks, it's now too late to get in on the ground floor. The fortunes will be made by people who already own all the land over there.

That's not true, of course, as any knowledgeable investor (or reader of this book) will know. Some people, to be sure, were in on the ground floor. They include people who have owned land there for years, plus the inevitable few with political influence who were secretly tipped off to the bridge coming and bought before the public announcement.

You know, however, from chapter 5, that this public announcement really signals the first of the three best times to buy land: when something is going to happen. Now that the news is out, much land will quickly come on the market from owners who wish to sell while the selling is good. They're taking no chances. They immediately boost the price of the land and sell out. They'll get double or triple, perhaps more, than the price of their land prior to that story spilling

99

the news in the paper. That's great with them, they figure. They sell fast, and run off with their new-found money.

If the news is true and if the bridge is built, they could wait, however, and turn over their land profits ten to twenty times as much, and not just by an extra few hundred dollars, or possibly a thousand dollars or two. They merely have to bide their time; their land will undoubtedly soar in value. The smart investor knows this, so he realizes that now could be a very good time for action.

The very first action is to confirm the facts of that story. Is it all true? Will the bridge be built where the story says? What about other details given in the story?

As nearly every person knows merely from reading news stories about his own business or profession, what you read in the paper is not always notable for its accuracy, to put it mildly. To verify such a story you read or hear, go to the central source, the horse's mouth. Call the state or local highway department, or both. If a federal highway grant is to be made for the bridge and its approach roads, track down their official release written on the matter. Write, for example, to the U.S. Department of Transportation, Washington, D.C. 20590, or to your congressman for it. Among other things, you also will want a copy of the official map of the bridge location and proposed highway links. If you're working with a good real estate broker, much of this research effort may be unnecessary because he will make it his business to get such information. You would do well, however, to make copies of his research material.

The big point, summed up: For basic facts to go to the central source. Don't rely on secondhand information. For one thing, plain common sense calls for checking facts at their source. For another, obtaining the official public announcements and other such papers about a new development can provide you with certain facts not given in a condensed news story. One or more could put a deeper, more revealing light on the development. Uncovering that easily obtainable fundamental research automatically lifts you to a level a mile above most other potential investors. It makes you the one person in five hundred really well armed with the facts, which can give you a head start on other potential investors.

Eight basic research sources

Once you decide to invest in land, and long before news of a big development comes, it will pay to begin building your own little fact bank of basic research. What are the growth predictions for the area you're interested in? What kind of growth? Where will it hit hardest? What about the population forecasts for the future? Good answers to questions like these and much else can be had from one or more of the following sources:

1. *Your local planning department.* Sometimes it's the "Planning Commission." It's usually a town- or county level agency with the job of helping public officials plan and build for the future. Hence the planning department is involved every day in future growth needs, where new roads and highways may be needed, provisions required to satisfy future needs for such things as jobs and housing, as well as expanded public services.

Not every locality, to be sure, has its own local planning department, and those that do exist are by no means all of high caliber. They range from excellent to poor. Nearly every one issues periodic public reports, including usually an annual report on local growth. Obviously, it's something to get. Also check on your state's planning department, especially if there's no local planning department. For research above and beyond the call of the duty, get to know the head of the planning department, or the director of research. You might even take one of them out to a relaxed social lunch once in a while. That also goes for knowledgeable officials in the research groups that follow. That's called casting bread upon the waters.

2. *Your Regional Planning Association.* For the New York metropolitan area it's the Tri-State Regional Plan Association, which has headquarters in New York City. In Philadelphia, it's the Delaware Valley Regional Planning Association. In Chicago, it's the Northeast Illinois Regional Planning Association. Whatever it's called in your area, its plans today could have a major impact on your land use tomorrow.

There is or will be a quasi-government regional planning group like these in nearly every part of the nation because federal law now requires one before federal grants and other aid will be made for related public projects. Some of these groups will surely exert strong influence on local growth, others may be merely rubber-stamp machines. It's up to you to find out which kind you have and how important it is to keep in touch with its activities. All that may require is getting on its mailing list.

There are fewer private, regional plan associations than public ones, but new ones are being formed. Two relatively new ones are the Regional Plan Association of Los Angeles and the Metropolitan Fund in Detroit. Probably the biggest, oldest, and most influential of all is New York's Regional Plan Association, 235 East 45th Street, N.Y. 10017, a nonprofit research and study group seriously concerned with growth within roughly a 100-mile radius of New York City. Individual membership is only $15 a year, for which you get its newsletters and reports on its various studies. This could pay off well.

I mentioned earlier, for example, that one of its studies, released in early 1974, discounted the need for a fourth New York jetport, partly because jumbo jets coupled with the energy crisis were sharply reducing the number of airplane flights required to handle the city's air-travel needs. It called for a serious reexamination of the plan to expand Stewart Airport, near West Point, N.Y., into New York's fourth major jetport. By being a $15-a-year member of the New York Regional Plan Association, anyone planning to invest in land near that potential jetport would have been alerted to that study being launched. You also, possibly, could have been alerted in advance to its probable conclusion. Find out about the likelihood of a similar group in your area, and obviously, if there is one, get to know it.

3. *The SMSA figures for your area.* SMSA stands for Standard Metropolitan Statistical Area. At last count there were some 268 such large and medium-large metropolitan areas in the country, including Puerto Rico. That's according to the U.S. Department of Commerce, which classifies an SMSA as an area with at least one or two cities with a total population of 50,000 people or more.

Together with the Bureau of the Census, the Department of Commerce keeps running tabs on practically every important and sometimes not-so-important social and economic fact about each such geographical area, down to the number of babies and grownups, type of work, housing, and much else short of the number of redheads with blue eyes.

In short, this basic source can be invaluable. If necessary, call on a local librarian to help you understand it. SMSA data for your area usually can be had by a call or letter to the nearest U.S. Department of Commerce or Bureau of the Census office. Or write to the Bureau of the Census, Social and Economics Statistics Administration, Washington, D.C. 20233.

4. *The Urban Land Institute,* 1200 18th Street NW, Washington, D.C. 20036. This national nonprofit group was originally the baby of a group of national real estate people concerned with good land planning and use for all purposes. (Yes, some real estate people can be practically altruistic.) It has grown since, and besides many top national real estate developers and brokers among its members, many other kinds of people concerned with land are also officers and members. It puts out a monthly newsletter that reports news and developments in land. It also sponsors seminars in different parts of the country, and undertakes studies on various facets of its multifaceted subject. It's an excellent source for keeping up to date on land. Individual membership dues are $85 a year; $40 for teachers, students, and libraries. Its monthly publication, *Urban Land* can be had for $15 a year.

5. *Ten-cent local sources.* The information you get can be worth considerably more. Ten cents is the cost of a phone call to the publisher of the local newspaper, the gas or electric utility public relations director, and the Chamber of Commerce (though it may go to 20 cents soon). Each has obvious good reasons to sing the praises of its area, and generally each will also have a handout information packet on the rosy local growth prospects and the countless reasons it's in one of God's favored areas.

That's par for the course for such material but still here and there in their free packets some excellent information is often buried. They also contain good leads to where you can find facts you need.

Information from your utility company, in particular, could be indicative of future growth face in the area. That's simply because a utility must put out big money well ahead of time to expand its power capacity. It must get new power lines started today out to the location of tomorrow's new business, industry, and housing. Each will be calling for instant power when new people begin moving in every month. Where are they betting on the greatest growth? The answer is often cited in the material they hand out or in their annual reports. Should you have a pertinent question about a particular area, make another call to the utility. For example, how much increased future power demand do they predict for the area?

6. *The League of Women Voters.* This is a sleeper, and worth still another phone call. Ask for their directory of information for voters. It may not be as plentiful with facts and figures as what you get from the Chamber of Commerce, but the League's information could be less susceptible to puffing and contain some good basic data about your area.

7. *Private real estate consultants and counselors.* No big investor in his right mind will put money into land without first getting an expert's advice on the deal. Developers also use the same experts to check things before they buy.

Because economics, like nature, abhors a vacuum, a whole breed of research consultants and counselors has sprung up to provide the new mousetrap for research facts, studies, and special knowledge about land. True, hiring one can cost money. But some will provide advice and consultation requiring limited work and effort on their part for a comparatively small fee, especially if a full-fledged study is not required. One of the more highly regarded such consultants is the Real Estate Research Corporation, with headquarters in Chicago and branch offices in a number of other cities. Another is Homer Hoyt Associates in Washington, D.C.

Others come in a variety of sizes, shapes, and price tags for their services. They include one-man counselors in large cities and small towns, as well as those with an office staff of economists and researchers. Their fees can run as low as $40 an hour, or about $300 to $500 a day to check property for you, up to a specified custom fee for performing a more complete research check for you. Talk to a few. There's no charge merely to meet a counselor for initial discussion.

You can get a list of some of the most professional ones in the business from the American Society of Real Estate Counselors, 155 East Superior Street, Chicago, Illinois 60611. Some real estate brokers also offer professional counseling, but the quality of advice you get depends, naturally, on the broker. One kind of counselor who should raise a caution flag before your eyes is the man or woman who offers counseling with one hand and promotes land investment deals with the other. He should be viewed with caution because of the potential conflict of interest. Which master is he serving?

8. *The Department of Agriculture.* This is another sleeper

source, except for smart investors who frequently call on the local office for information about land. Merely tell them what you want and why, and their people generally will respond with exceedingly helpful answers. The county agent for the area can also be one of the very best of all individual sources about the local land and its characteristics.

chapter 10

HOW TO JUDGE
LAND

Now let's say you've done your homework. You've gone shopping and found some land you may buy. How good is it? How do you tell? How should it be inspected and checked? You hire an expert to check it for you—though it usually takes several different experts. Or you're dealing with a good broker who swears, right hand up, that the land scores top marks in every category.

No matter. A personal inspection by you is still mandatory. Its importance cannot be overemphasized if only because very few people look on water to be crossed with the same view of he who must make the crossing.

So you visit the site and walk it back and forth and around its borders. You check its drainage characteristics after a heavy rain, which should be, if at all possible, in spring or fall. What is dry as the Sahara in August could be knee deep in water in April. Take pictures of the site, and also of the surrounding land.

While there, discreetly talk to neighbors and others who live and work close by. You need only discuss the time of day with them, or if necessary, say that you're considering buying property in the area, and you'd like to know anything they'll tell you. For example, is it really good land? What about flooding problems? Ask a few leading questions and most people will talk at length. A spate of interesting information could come your way.

Here are other specific points to check:

Accessibility

Does the site have ample road frontage on a good public road or highway? Take a copy of the property map with you and double check the road frontage. See for yourself the kind of accessibility to be sure that it is good. If there is little or no road frontage, beware. Poor accessibility is one of the most common of all traps to avoid when buying land.

One man, for example, bought an appealing corner plot of land that was zoned for commercial use and was, it seemed, an excellent site for new stores. Both a main highway and a good minor road were nearby. The land was reasonably priced and the man had to fight back his enthusiasm over being able to buy it. After buying, however, he discovered that his newly bought corner site had no right of access to the principal road and only limited access on the minor road. No wonder the bargain price. He had clearly not really checked the site's accessibility.

A good real estate lawyer should be called on to be sure that no legal booby trap prevents accessibility. Besides, you'll probably need a lawyer to check other legal facts, such as the possibility of a title snag or easement problem. If you don't trust lawyers, simply put a blanket statement in your sales contract saying that the seller guarantees that no hidden snags exist, and you have each one spelled out. If there are any, your purchase is voided. That, alas, is easier said than done, because of the complicated way lawyers have written our real estate laws.

Besides direct accessibility into and out of the property from a main road or highway, what about accessibility from it to the outside world? That means to the nearest metropolitan area, housing and shopping centers, closest superhighway, railroad, and so on. The order of priorities for these depends on the land's use.

Land for commercial use

If the land is to be used commercially, the following site features rate highest, according to Jerome S. Sverdlick, a New York lawyer who has been active in real estate for more than twenty-five years.

•   Good transportation to a main highway. Public transportation to and from the site will usually mean a superior site, thus higher value in the market place.

•   Utilities. Each one necessary clearly must be obtainable. That means, of course, water, electricity, sewer line, storm sewer, and gas or steam energy. These latter two—gas and steam—may be unnecessary if ample electricity can be had at not too high a cost for winter heating. What about the cost to bring each in?

•   Labor. Can the other business firms that settle in draw on an ample labor supply in the area around? If not, good public transportation may be essential to insure getting workers to work.

•   What about customers? This is a major requirement, naturally, to keep retail stores on the site in business. Are there enough potential customers in the area to support the stores you envision?

Various criteria are used to determine the minimum number of people nearby (market area) required to support stores. Moreover, crowds of marketing experts and consultants will leap at the chance to determine market area facts for a site. As a rule, the primary trading area for a small neighborhood shopping center is determined by the appeal of the king store in it, usually a supermarket. Besides the supermarket usually needed to anchor a small center, there generally will also be a drugstore, a variety store, and a hardware store. From 70 to 90 percent of the people using the shopping center will be pulled there by the supermarket. Most generally come from an area roughly two to three miles away along the major roads serving the center.

There's more to it than that, of course, and any smart supermarket operator can quickly check the feasibility of a new site for a profitable new store. He'll consider the nearest competition that will bear on his sales. Traffic counts on the nearest roads are often required to determine the potential market. Among other things, does the site have sufficient parking area for customers' cars?

By now you've got the idea. Putting a lot of money into developing land for a major use is no simple matter. But the more such data, you, the potential land buyer-owner, can amass in advance, the greater the likelihood that you will profit.

Land for industrial use

For good transportation, a heart-blood requirement for most industry, the site should be located conveniently near a superhighway or expressway, and also perhaps to a railroad line, an airport, and possibly a seaport, depending on the kind of industrial use.

Utilities may require a good source of industrial water plus the means to get rid of industrial waste. That's in addition to the basic requirements for water, electricity, and sewage disposal. Labor requirements can call for a pool of skilled labor nearby, as well as for executives, engineers and so on within commuting distance. Public transportation may be somewhat less important for an industrial center but still may be vital.

Land for residential use

The following features are important in this order, according to Sverdlick:

Transportation
Shopping nearby
Schools
Churches
Jobs
Recreational facilities and parks
Utilities
Nuisance neighbors (factory, railroad, noisy highway, airport, etc.),

The different classes of land

Land has been classified into eight different categories of use by the U.S. Department of Agriculture. These range from Class I, with virtually ideal soil and other characteristics in decreasing order of quality, down to Class VIII, with the severest limiting features. The particular classification of land can also give a good indication of the suitability of land for other, nonagricultural use. It can tell you, for example, about the drainage characteristics of land, so important for virtually any kind of construction, and about subsoil traits that can also have a strong influence on the use of land. Obviously, knowing how land is classified can inform you about its basic quality and its value, per se, even though the way land is classified may seem to apply chiefly to farmers, ranchers, and forestry people.

The first four classes of land, Class I to Class IV, rate land in decreasing order of its suitability for growing most common crops. Class I has nearly ideal soil, is deep and well drained, and is least susceptible to wind or water erosion. Classes II to IV have more limitations and less good soil, with Class III having severe limitations for most crops making it marginal farmland.

Classes V to VII are generally unsuitable for field crops and limited to grazing or forestry uses in descending order of quality. Class V would be best for these uses, Class VII worst because of such drawbacks as very steep slopes, rocky terrain, or excessive erosion.

Class VIII, the least desirable of all land, can sometimes be reclaimed with the proper treatment. It's usually tough land to deal with however, because of such major drawbacks as rock outcrops and mine tailings, or it is sheer badlands.

To determine the classification of land you may be interested in, talk to the people at the nearest Soil Conservation Service office of the Department of Agriculture. Or call on the county agent for the area. Also write to the Department of Agriculture, Washington, D.C. 20250, for its booklet, number PA–128, "The Measure of Our Land."

How much is the land worth?

What price, really, is a particular site worth? How much should you pay for it? As little as possible, of course. Actually, you should know three things: what it's likely to be worth in the future when you may sell, its value today, and the top price that you should pay for it today.

The usual way to estimate present-day market value is by a professional appraisal by a good real estate appraiser. Sometimes you may want two appraisals from two different appraisers. Just as the value of a used house is estimated by the most recent sales prices of comparable houses in the neighborhood, the value of land is judged largely by the same "comparison" method.

Brokers are fond of using this approach. Showing your acreage, a broker will say, for example, "That parcel over there to the north just sold six months ago for $4,800 an acre. Turning around, he'll mention "that piece on the south sold for $5,000 an acre only two months ago." Then earnestly to you he'll say, "So you see, this land right here is a steal at $4,500 an acre! You can't pass it up, or it'll be gone tomorrow."

Comparable sales, however, are not necessarily the last word. Recent comparable sales of property could be out of line in either direction because of swift new developments in the area. They could be social or political, as well as economic. You must determine their existence and their impact on present and future land values. A good appraiser or broker on his toes can help here, but don't assume such advice.

Determining the future value of land

How this, the next step, is done can be illustrated by the twenty-acre farm west of Chicago, mentioned in Chapter 5, that was bought for $10,000 an acre in 1973. Its buyers figured that its value would climb to $40,000 an acre within five years. That $40,000 figure is no mere fantasy.

It was estimated according to the precept that "equal time means equal land prices," in the words of Lawrence D. Elkind, a developer of industrial parks and shopping centers. He emphasizes, however, that this is by no means an infallible way to gauge future value. But it has long been the best general way to estimate future value.

It holds that raw land today will be worth tomorrow roughly the same as the value today of other, nearby developed land having equal traveling time from the same central business district. Other land comparable to that twenty-acre farm elsewhere in Chicago but in use and located within another comparable expressway corridor was worth roughly $40,000 an acre in 1973. Thus after the new expressway going past this farm is completed, comparable land here should be worth the same, in other words, $40,000 an acre. That's based, by the way, on 1973 dollars.

Similarly, a parcel of land you're viewing may be forty minutes travel time from downtown, or will be in the future when a new highway is completed. Its value then, therefore, should be about the same as the value of other developed land in your metropolitan area

Class I land is lush and virtually ideal for common crops. It holds water well, is well drained and is subject to a minimum of wind or water erosion. (*U.S.D.A.* Photograph)

This Class II land is vulnerable to erosion, To prevent it, contouring and stripcropping conservation is practiced. (*U.S.D.A.* Photograph)

Class III land is subject to wetness, if not total flooding, and drainage must be provided. An exception is a crop that may require water, like rice. (*U.S.D.A.* Photograph)

This is an example of Class IV land which is level or gently sloping. Its soil will generally not erode but is too wet to be practical for many crops. It is largely restricted to use as pasture or range land. (*U.S.D.A.* Photograph)

This is Class V land because its soil is largely unsuitable for most crops. Given the right climate and rainfall, it can be used for meadows, or like this, for an orchard. (*U.S.D.A.* Photograph)

Sheep are grazing here on an example of Class VI land that is suitable for such use. Land rising in the background has Class VII soil. (*U.S.D.A.* Photograph)

used today for the same purpose envisioned for your land.

The nearest metropolitan downtown area is the focal point for the comparison because it's generally the focal point for the area jobs, as well as being the commercial center for an area. Jobs are the key attraction, the raison d'être for most population centers.

Sometimes the surrounding suburbs grow so fast that the central city is no longer the overwhelmingly central job magnet. More and more people may find work elsewhere in the suburbs. This has become increasingly true in recent years, and as a result the "equal time" accessibility to the downtown business district of some areas may no longer exert the same pulling power and influence on surrounding land values as before. Nevertheless, the distance to your metropolitan downtown "is still an important factor," still the most important influence, according to Alan R. Winger, Professor of Economics in the College of Business Administration, University of Florida. That's especially true for land to be used for new housing.

Other elements can also enter the picture, especially because no two tracts of land are identical in all ways. A tract could be blessed with features that make it worth more than comparable land of "equal time" from downtown. It may have especially good frontage on a main highway, or excel for luxury housing, or whatever. Then you might jack up its value accordingly. On the other hand, it may be cursed in a way that is tough to correct. Then you jack down its value accordingly. Look at the whole picture realistically and don't kid yourself. And then, whatever the case, play safe. Mark down the projected future value by a contingency figure of about 10 to 20 percent.

How much should you pay?

This is the vital third step, determining the top price that you should pay for land. It's the maximum price to pay that will leave enough cushion between it and your selling price later so that the land grows in value by at least 15 to 20 percent a year compounded. If it cannot increase in value by that much nowadays, you would be wise to forget it. You would do equally well after taxes by putting your money elsewhere.

That top allowable purchase price is determined by working backward. Say, for example, that you have your eye on land that is priced today at $2,000 an acre for ten acres for sale, or $20,000. You figure (step two above) that it will double in price in six or seven years, and you could sell it then for $40,000. Should you buy it now? (That $40,000 future value is based on present day values and the present-day dollar. That should automatically take future inflation into account.)

The answer is no. A compound interest table will tell you that doubling in price in six years will mean a return of only 12 percent a year before taxes and all other expenses. For a minimum return of 15 percent a year, you must buy the land now for no more than $17,300, or $1,730 an acre. If it takes seven years before you can sell for $40,000 and earn you at least 15 percent a year, you would have to buy today for no more than $15,000.

That's how to figure back to the maximum price you should pay today for land. Depending on your personal needs and your feelings about the investment, other assumptions can be made. You might boost your minimum acceptable return to at least 20 percent a year, or lower it below 15 percent.

In addition, you would obviously zero-in closely on other relevant variables that will influence the decision. What will the actual total annual ownership costs be (for taxes, insurance, financing charges, etc.)? On the positive side, how much leverage can you exert with a low cash down payment? Your income tax bracket comes into play here, of course, as well as being an influence on other figures. The table on pages 62–65, showing after-tax returns on various land investments, can be of help here.

Actually, a really good land purchase will be fairly obvious to the tutored eye. At the very least, it should be very likely to double in value within four to five years; or, triple in value within six to seven years; or, quadruple in value within eight to ten years.

Anything less than that likely promise should be viewed with skepticism. Life is too short to waste time and money on borderline land, and especially that which may not give a return of at least 15 percent or so a year compounded. That's a meager return in the mid-1970s, though it could be a good return in the future should interest rates decline.

Putting it another way, when you find that you are pondering back and forth whether land for sale is worth buying, that's often good reason to decline it. If in doubt, don't. And should a real question about whether land is a good buy exist in your mind, often you can find the answer in your own feelings about the land. That's assuming that you have done your homework, including determining what the land will be worth at year x in the future. Then probe your basic feelings toward the land. Is there still real doubt about buying it? If so, don't buy.

But the land may nag you. You still feel it's too good to pass up. Then figure how much lower the purchase price should be before it is worth purchasing. Shave a little more off that price, offer it to the seller, and that's that. You may be surprised at how quickly a seller will accept a price lower than you thought he would. Sometimes he will not, to be sure. Then your consolation is that there's other good land around available at a good price and no doubt about its future.

chapter 11

KNOW THY SELLER

Now comes the moment of truth. You've examined the merchandise and made a choice. But unlike paying a fixed price at the checkout counter, the purchase generally calls for verbal sparring and much give and take between buyer and seller. You're two antagonists in a ring. There can be more at stake now than at any other time during the process of shopping and buying (except possibly later when you negotiate a second time to sell).

According to the conventional wisdom, you will, of course, remain cool, collected, and unemotional, though actually an honest show of pent-up emotion once in a while is perfectly understandable. A seasoned labor management negotiator will say that a calculated very low first bid when you're buying can be a good ploy. The lower the initial bid, the greater the likelihood that it will pull down the final price the buyer will accept. Your subsequent bids may have to be raised, to be sure. Nonetheless, a low first bid can exert a psychological softening impact on the seller, making him more susceptible to reducing his price more than he would have otherwise.

Conversely, if you're selling, the higher your first asking price, the higher the sales price you're likely to receive. It also gives you a greater bargaining cushion on the up side for coming down in price, as necessary. The same principle generally holds when you negotiate a salary for a new job as well, and when you buy or sell almost anything else not subject to a fixed price, as any wily Arabian bazaar merchant will tell you.

But you should not overdo it, of course. There's a limit to how far you may go, high or low, without overplaying your hand. Submitting a ridiculously low first bid will insult some sellers. (A broker must by law deliver to the seller whatever bid you insist on, even though he may think it inadvisable.) If you place a ridiculously high asking price on merchandise for sale you can lose more than you gain.

Overpricing is, for example, one of the most frequent mistakes made by people selling their own houses. They put houses on the market at wildly high sales prices. It happens all the time, and it's why so many houses often go unsold for so much time. The over-priced house is commonly passed over by people who might otherwise buy it at a realistic price. Something about an overpriced house also puts a stigma on it, and often it goes unsold for long afterward. Then it's sold at a much reduced price that's considerably less than could have been obtained earlier if the house had been priced realistically. The same thing can happen in land.

Negotiation is an art and as a result there are no set rules for it. Like research analysis, you must have a feel for it. Or have a good broker perform for you. The essential starting point in either case is to have done your homework and have a pretty good reading on the market value of land for sale. Then comes knowledge and understanding of the seller. How long has he owned the land? Why is he selling now? Is he forced to sell?

Some of the answers can be readily had by looking up the land deed and its title history at the county courthouse. Some of it can also be learned merely by asking. Not every owner, of course, will necessarily submit truthful answers. But you can never tell.

The most common sellers

Go shopping for land and you will find that most owners with land for sale will fall into certain common categories. They range from the farmer on the one extreme to the speculator on the other. The most common sellers have been listed, as follows, by Nathan J. Miller, president of Building and Land Technology, Inc., Paramus, New

Jersey, a firm that specializes in the acquisition of raw land for home builders and other developers and in improving land for use.

Miller is a former home builder with, in all, more than twenty years of experience seeking land for sale and dealing with almost all kinds of sellers you will meet in the marketplace. He has some cogent advice about how to deal with the most common sellers you're likely to encounter. Who they are, some of their typical behavior traits, and what you might expect dealing with each were detailed for me by Miller in a long interview that I had with him; I have also drawn material from an article about his views published in *House & Home*, the professional home-building journal.* Because Miller is a professional buyer of land for development, much of the following is based on his experiences shopping for land that is ready for development. Nonetheless, his encounters with various sellers still hold instructive lessons for others who shop earlier in the game for land that may not yet be ready for development.

The farmer

The working farmer is the prime source of large parcels of land, according to Miller. But finding such land and the farmer who has it for sale can require more than watching for his ads in the paper or traveling the country roads looking for "For Sale" signs on the land. Once you've met up with a farmer with land for sale, you may still have a long way to go before you sit down at the kitchen table to negotiate with him. More than a few letters or phone calls to him may be necessary. You and or your broker, or both of you, often must knock on his farmhouse door, understand his motives, and persuade him to sell. Sometimes you must establish a good persuasive case for him to sell at a reasonable price and reasonable conditions.

Consider his background. Usually, he's worked the farm for years, and now has good reason to sell. Once you've established rapport with him he's usually easy to deal with. He's worked hard to make a living, often a bare living, at one of the toughest of all occupations. Year in and year out he's been dependent on unpredictable

*June R. Vollman, "How to Find Raw Land in the Right Place and How to Make the Best Deal," *House & Home* (August 1972), copyright 1972 by McGraw-Hill Inc. The material in this chapter is used with permission of *House & Home*, but in different form from its original publication.

weather, fluctuating prices, and the other uncertainties of farming. While he doesn't have to worry about food and a roof over his head (though sometimes it can be leaky), often he has accumulated little cash. His farm will generally represent his total wealth, the capital earned from a lifetime of labor.

Now a buyer for his land comes along and the farmer sees his first real chance to get his hands on big money. His taxes will not be too high because the sale will represent a long-term capital gain. To be sure, some farmers have done well, by dint of luck, chance, hard work, or a combination of all three. As a result they could well have a tidy cash reserve to fall back on, in addition to their farm. This kind of farmer may be less inclined to sell except at an unreasonably high price.

If he's weary of farming or if he's inherited the land and doesn't like to farm, a good sale will free him to find other work or simply let him head south and retire. If he likes farming, before the contract ink is dry he can go twenty miles farther out and buy a new place to farm for part of the money received for his old one and salt away the rest.

However good a reason to sell a farmer has, don't expect just to walk in and make a deal on your own terms. Most farmers are well aware of the value of their land, especially if it is to be rezoned and made ready for development. That's particularly the case when suburban sprawl is rapidly catching up to his land, or in other words, after his land has entered its predeveloped stage and its value has begun to climb.

Other farmers, in areas beyond the first thrust of approaching suburbia, may be ready to sell before their land is ready for development. The farmer who suddenly reads in the paper that a new bridge will open up his part of the country, or that a new airport or expressway is coming, has sudden visions (in living color, of course) of financial glory. As I noted earlier, he might demand and deserve a price three to four times the value of his land the night before, and he will be doing well. (But should the reported new development go through, the land's value could multiply considerably more within a few years.)

To forestall unreasonable demands, you might recommend that he hire a lawyer to advise him on the realities of land values. He will learn, for example, that he must pay taxes on the entire sale if he takes more than 30 percent of the price in cash during the first calendar year. The initial payment to him generally will range down to 10 percent, the lowest down payment likely to be acceptable if the farmer thinks you are strong financially. Then he'll take a mortgage from you at a somewhat higher interest rate than he could get at the savings bank.

If the time is close when the land can be developed and built on, the sale could hinge on obtaining a zoning change for it. The farmer may not borrow against the purchase contract. Then he must be paid for taking his land off the market for a period. This could take the form of a sweetener like nonreturnable option money, or a higher purchase price.

The negotiations of a builder or other developer with a farmer will go something like this, according to Miller:

Say a 100-acre farm is worth $1,000 an acre, the price a speculator would pay for it. I try to persuade a farmer who is selling that during the option time I will invest the time, money and talent necessary to create a subdivision, or a site plan, a PUD [Planned Unit Development] or whatever for a farm. I will say, "right now a speculator would pay you $100,000 for this land. But if you ride along with me you can get $130,000, or as much as $150,000."

It won't cost him a penny, and he'll still be able to farm his land. I'll do no more than make some test borings that don't disturb his work. His only risk is holding the land off the market. If the sale falls through, his land will still be worth $100,000 and probably more, considering what's happening to the price of farmland. So he's made a good deal for himself.

Other sweeteners that professional land buyers and developers use include a flexible option with renewals at stated intervals and a higher price after each renewal. Sometimes there's a monthly penalty for each month the option goes past a specified date. But, of course, there must be a final cut-off time.

It may be difficult to come to terms with a farmer because he lives in a small community where a few farmers own most of the land. He'll talk about his deal with his neighbors and possibly get an inflated idea of the value of his property, and then things can get difficult. At times there can be a basic uneasiness—not distrust particularly, but more of a wariness—between the farmer with land to sell and the speculator, city slicker, or developer coming out to buy "our farm." Then a farmer may get cautious and think, "Maybe I better wait and let him buy my neighbor's place."

A farmer understandably has a strong emotional tie to the soil, especially when the farm came to him from his father. If the farmer has a large family, everyone in it may have a different idea of the property's worth. Sometimes a town has built up around his farm, and the people in town don't want to see the farm go.

Sometimes a crafty farmer wants to sell at the top of the market but has no intention of giving up farming. Miller calls him the country slicker. He is personified by one wily operator who put his dairy farm, outside Princeton, New Jersey, up for sale a few years ago. It was the largest farm in a rapidly growing area. Miller made an offer to buy the farm, but he says:

> Both the farmer and his lawyer were very sharp and the negotiations dragged on and on. We agreed on money terms, but I could never get the farmer to sign on the dotted line.
>
> No matter what additional demands I agreed to, the farmer raised another objection, and still another. For example, he loved his work, and so did his wife. Then they wanted their son, who had just been graduated from Rutgers, to have at least a year and a half's experience running the farm. Then I agreed that they could use the farm for a period after the deal went through.
>
> What I didn't know but subsequently discovered was that all the stalling stemmed from negotiations the farmer was having for still another piece of land about thirty miles farther out. It was priced at about 10 percent of what I was paying him. I thought I was making a good deal, and I was.
>
> I then learned that this was the fourth time the farmer had worked the same deal. He had only owned the farm I was buying for ten years. From the start I had thought that he was negotiating and renegotiating for the best available terms, but in reality he was setting himself up for the next killing.

The builder-developer

Next to the working farmer, the builder-developer, of all people, ranks right up there among the best sources of land for sale. Often he has bitten off more land than he can chew and he must sell to get out of a cash bind. Given the sharp boom-and-bust nature of the home-building business, a builder often finds himself land poor when the business is slumping. So he needs the money obtainable from a land sale. Besides, land by itself is a primary business with the builder-developer. He's always in and out of it, and there's probably more buying and selling among builders and developers than among any other group.

Other reasons that prompt him to sell will make him less desperate. By virtue of his building, an adjacent piece of property may represent a greater profit to him by selling it than by building on it. The land could be good for apartments, but he's chiefly a small-house builder. Or it's now a natural for a shopping center, again something that's not his cup of tea. So he decides to sell.

Is it difficult to deal with a builder or developer? Not every developer, by the way, is also a builder, or vice versa. (The two may be the same person, or two different breeds.) Still, the decision to sell depends on his financial situation and his need to sell. If it's a forced sale to raise cash, he will obviously want the highest possible sales price, but he'll be realistic and take any reasonable offer.

On the other hand, if he thinks he has a choice property that's ready for a killing and he isn't forced to sell, watch out, says Miller. He'll wheel and deal for the highest possible price and profit, and look down his nose at anything less.

The smaller builder, however, tends to be more flexible than the large builder. If a small builder can make a few bucks by selling some land that has appreciated in value, he will do it. Often he'll build the first ten or twenty houses in a subdivision, and then sell the rest of the land. That, by the way, is how many a professional becomes a land dealer or developer. He starts out as a home builder but soon learns that building houses is a tough business loaded with pitfalls. But—lo and behold—considerable money can be made with fewer problems merely by buying raw land and making it ready for building. In other words, he buys and improves land, and then, he figures, he'll unload it on some fool who builds houses because he doesn't know better.

The gentleman farmer

This seller often has much land for sale at a high price. But unlike the working farmer in overalls, he can be one of the toughest sellers to deal with. Sometimes he's just impossible, because he owns the farm for tax reasons or as a weekend retreat rather than as a means of obtaining his livelihood. The gentleman farmer usually has a lot of money. Cash is no problem to him; he doesn't have to sell. He often has a tenant farmer working the land for him. But he may sell if he can't get a good tenant farmer or grows tired of the farm. One such owner, at age eighty-five, found that he visited his property only once or twice a year; he decided that he might sell. Each time a sale was imminent, however, he backed out at the last moment, always behaving as though he was going to live another fifty years.

Dealing with such a seller, you must sense whether or not he is really serious and will sell. He may not sell today, but if you really want his land, you call him again in a month or two. Such sales are often made because a buyer doesn't give up, or because the owner does decide to sell and feels obligated to one who has pursued him. Because a gentleman farmer generally doesn't need the money, an option situation can be a good thing to prompt the sale. You say, "I will pay you x dollars for an option to buy the land." After a year, or whatever the period cited, you have the option to buy the land at a stipulated price. If you still want the land when the time is up, you follow through and buy at the price. If a sale isn't made, the seller pockets the option money and keeps the land.

Estate land

The owner has died and his land passes on to his heirs and they decide to sell, only it's not always that simple. Often the land must be sold to obtain money needed to pay inheritance taxes and meet other estate expenses. Because things were left to the last minute, the money is often needed quickly as the tax deadline looms dead ahead. Timing therefore can be crucial, and you have to work fast.

A large cash down payment, however, may be required because of the money required to pay the estate obligations. This could kill the deal for some buyers, but on the other hand it could work for you. By eliminating other potential bidders for the land, and assuming you can afford the high down payment required, it could give you a strong bargaining lever that will mean better terms, including a reduced sales price.

Another advantage in dealing for estate land is that the negotiations are generally carried out with a lawyer or two or a banker, the typical executors who are professionals. They don't toss unnecessary roadblocks in your way. They are concerned chiefly with consummating a reasonable deal as quickly as possible. Thus once the executor decides that the land should be sold, negotiations proceed smoothly. But the negotiations must revolve around conditions that will solve the estate problems, a prime concern.

The negotiations take on another color, however, if you must deal with an executor or trustee who is also a member of the family. Then a variety of roadblocks can be thrown in the way, especially if there are several heirs to the property. Each heir has his own great idea of how the land should be sold and the price it should bring. Or no one can make a decision without consulting everyone else—and everyone else will seldom agree. If you truly want the land and you are indefatigable, you could still get it, as shown by one of Miller's negotiations for land with a classic group of battling heirs:

This wasn't a case of wheeling and dealing; it was a problem of animosity. The property was part of an estate that went back twenty-five or thirty years, and the executors were two attorneys and one principal. When it finally came time to sign the contract, they asked me to a meeting.

I found myself face-to-face with some thirty people, all different members of one family and all were heirs, down to grandchildren and maybe great-grandchildren. But a lot of these relatives weren't talking to each other. They were sore at one another to begin with, and they hadn't seen each other for years, during which time they became even sorer. It took meetings over two long holiday weekends to bring the deal off.

At the beginning I thought I was dealing with only three trustees. I figured it would only take eight or nine days to get to contract. But with all those heirs in the act, it wound up taking eight or nine months to work out the deal. I was lucky to wind up with any kind of contract.

Other estate land for sale can be impossible to buy because there is no will, or an heir is missing. This can put a snag in the title that can't be blotted out. It happens more often than people realize. If you face such a situation, recognize it for the tough nut it is, and by and large you'll do well to step out of the picture. On the another hand, remember that much good land often becomes available from estates. Sometimes you can obtain an inside track to it by letting lawyers know that you would be interested in such land when it becomes available. Then don't be surprised by a call about some good land for sale.

Government land

It's land that is no longer needed by city, town, state, or federal government. Anyone may buy it. There are also the supposedly vast tracks of virgin government land far from home that are believed (falsely) to be available dirt-cheap to any venturesome person. By and large, that's a myth. There's very little such land available, including virtually no more homesteading land, despite what slick mail-order promoters would have you think. And the little that is occasionally available must by law be sold at fair market value.

The government land frequently available is the local lot or two bought, say, for a new town garage that was never built, or other such purpose that didn't pan out. Or it's just plain surplus land. You'll see such parcels advertised in the small-print notices in the paper. But by that time a smart, early-bird investor will know all about it and have it practically sewed up. Nonetheless, by law such land must still be publicly offered and sold to the highest bidder.

The early bird, not waiting for such property to be offered, checks the tax rolls for public land that isn't used. Like anyone else, he has the right to submit a written offer to the town for it. The town, however, still must put the land up for public bids and sell only to the highest bidder. If you're early, however, you will have had time to check out the parcel, which could mean a head start over other buyers. For that matter, such land often could fall to you at your price because no one else bids on it.

Tax land

This is the property on which a municipal lien has been filed because the owner hasn't paid his taxes. This land is also advertised in the paper. If the taxes are not paid by a certain date, anyone may buy it for a sum equal to the unpaid taxes. Much of this tax property, however, is often listed but never available because some owners deliberately withhold their taxes till the last minute. So you should distinguish between this and genuine tax land that will be for sale.

There is also tax land whose ownership has already passed to the town by a foreclosure action. It generally can be bought, though it isn't necessarily offered for sale automatically. A would-be buyer may initiate a sale by making a bid for it the same way as noted above for surplus government land.

Other government land often for sale includes surplus land sold by the highway department or a turnpike commission because it's left over after a new road has been completed. Like all other public land, however, it may or may not be worth buying, depending on location, potential use and other such characteristics that determine the quality of land. Such things obviously should be checked before bidding.

If buying government land of one kind or another strikes your fancy, keep in touch with the public officials and employees, such as people in the highway department, who are concerned with such land. Bid on a piece offered, if only to learn the ropes. Protect yourself against being stuck by making a bid so low that it's sure to be rejected; if it's not, you get dirt-cheap land. Then later when something good comes up, you're no longer a neophyte bidding for it.

The large company not involved in housing

The land that comes on the market from this source usually is a very large tract and therefore requires a buyer with a good deal of money. It's usually land amassed by a company for investment purposes or for a future plant site that didn't materialize. The land becomes surplus, or the company executives simply decide it's a good time to sell and take their profit.

Negotiating with this seller depends, as with other sellers, on the company's need to sell and on the particular land and the price desired. Sometimes the land is ripe for development; if land development is not the company's business, its executives may look for a joint venture deal. A company official says, in effect, "We'll provide the land; you develop it, and we'll share the profit." But that restricts such salable land to a developer-buyer. The seller becomes a silent investor, the buyer sets the agreement parameters and goes on to develop the land. Many such joint ventures have, however, gone sour in recent years. So before anyone participates in one, as either buyer or seller, it's a good idea to be doubly sure about the likelihood of success.

Buying land from a big company as an investment, and not for development, will usually be a straightforward transaction preceded by hard bargaining. A company official or broker acting for the company will have the land appraised to determine its market value. Then he will sell for the best price offered, assuming it's close enough to the price desired.

The mortgage lender

He is still another source of what is usually a large, though not necessarily huge, tract of land for sale as a result of a building project going sour and the mortgage lender (bank, insurance company, mortgage broker, etc.) taking over the land by foreclosure. The usual lender is not in the land business, so he will turn around and sell the land at a price that will pay off the mortgage due him and bail him out. It's often land foreclosed on a home builder who has gone broke. Something went wrong, such as a lag in the economy, a bad estimate of the housing market, or very tight money—as happened notably, and disastrously, to many builders in 1974—and the builder could not weather the storm. The lender takes over and the land is put up for sale.

But this land is usually most suitable for another builder or developer who can complete its development, with exceptions. A smart investor could buy it when the underlying value is sound and future appreciation is a strong likelihood. You could then sell off that portion of the land where building may have been started to a builder who would complete that development. You hold the rest of the land for a later sale when it's more valuable. This can be a good investment because lenders are often the most reasonable of all sellers. They want their mortgage money back and will listen to any sound proposition to bail them out.

However, a lender stuck with such land may be partial to another builder because he, the lender, is interested in new business, too. Another builder taking over would mean a new construction loan to be issued on the property, as well as selling permanent mortgages later to the home buyers. Whether partial to a home-builder buyer or not, a lender will actively seek almost any buyer for land he's stuck with. So when you scout for land and talk to bankers and other mortgage lenders, tell them that you'd like to hear about such land if and when it is available.

The land speculator

This could be you a few years from now but you can cross that bridge later. The typical speculator is seldom a professional. He's more likely to be a doctor or businessman who by himself or together with others bought the land as an investment and is waiting for it to appreciate. Often it's a large tract bought at a good price but it still isn't ripe for development.

The owner, however, has held it long enough and would like to sell, at a profit, of course. He will advertise the land for sale and perhaps even put a sign on it. Sometimes he can be identified because simultaneously he will also have ads in the paper for more land to buy. In many small towns where everyone knows everyone else, the brokers will know who the land speculators are and which ones are now in the market to buy or sell.

The typical speculator is generally easy to deal with because he's had his land longer than anticipated, and now wants out. He'll also sell at a fair price, he says. But a fair price to him can be more than the land is really worth. On the other hand, he's generally receptive to negotiation. He will ease his terms if he can get a reasonably good price, and especially if he's assured of getting a good portion of his money from the land within a year or two. Besides, his ultimate aim always was to sell the land, not hold on to it forever. Incidentally, because he often buys land in an area that isn't ripe for development and it takes more time than anticipated for local development to reach his land, the speculator, often unknowingly, provides a service to society. He provides the essential land banking service for others, including future home buyers as well as those in the housing industry by buying up and holding land until it is ripe for development.

Other sellers

Other people with land for sale include the small-property owner and the subdivider and land sales company selling carved-up lots for vacation or retirement houses. To get an idea of the broad range of largely individual sellers, thumb through the national catalogs available free from such national brokerage firms as Strout Realty, Inc., P.O. Box 2757, Springfield, Mo. 65803, and United Farm Agency, 612

West 47th Street, Kansas City, Mo. 64112. As for the subdivider and land sales company, they are not for anyone seriously interested in investing in land. More on this later in chapter 14.

Summary

Nearly every seller will strive for the highest price and best terms he can get. (Naturally.) The more you can learn about a particular seller, the better for you. Here's when the negotiations can get interesting, and you could have fun, too. As a matter of fact, realize that it is a game in a way and there's no reason to be grim and humorless about it. Then you immediately start with an advantage. Besides, you can't win them all.

Determine that the land is a reasonably good buy, what it's worth, and the top price you're willing to pay. Then size up the seller. Inevitably, some will be downright obstinate and unreasonable. The sooner you see this and leave for greener pastures, the better. If the seller is reasonable, you simply start with a low bid and if necessary bounce the ball back and forth a few times. Raise your bid a few times up to the highest price you will pay. All along you weigh the seller's counter offers, reassess him as necessary, and strive to understand him as much as possible. Obviously. You seek that common ground that both can accept, and then you buy. True success is when both buyer and seller are satisfied.

chapter 12

HOW TO BUY LAND

The best way to buy land, says Alvin Arnold, editor of *The Real Estate Review,* is to team up with a local expert. He could be a real estate broker or a professional investor who specializes in setting up investments for others to participate in.

He knows about land as a result of buying and selling it. He knows the market for it. He's continually watching for a good buy, his antennae spread out all the time. Should a good opportunity present itself, he will generally call on people he knows to buy it with him. Besides investing his own money, he will also receive an extra share or two in the deal for his professional management of it.

Profile of a professional investor

An example is Albert Winnikoff, the Malibu, California, land investor and author of the book *The Land Game.* Not long after being graduated from the University of California in 1953 with a liberal arts degree, Winnikoff decided that land in southern California held great investment promise. He began a professional study of it as others might study philosophy. He practiced what he studied, buying and selling land. Now with more than twenty years of experience

133

under his belt as a land investor, and also as a real estate broker, he knows the land in his region like a surgeon knows the human body. He is always alert for a good new investment opportunity. When he comes on one he will generally call on a list of friends and business acquaintances to join him in buying a promising tract. But he is not unreceptive to those who may call out of the blue requesting that they be considered as partners in a future investment situation.

Men like Winnikoff can be found in many parts of the country. Some are real estate brokers, too, others not. Some may work at other professions but have a special talent for investing in land successfully. Each may work at it in his own way. To find a good one in your area, like a fisherman, you have to throw out a line or two.

Some, however, may not be so smart and honest as others. The ability of each to spot good land and judge it properly will vary, too. So when you encounter such a man you might invest with, it's up to you to size him up. Also, not to be minimized, he should be a man with whom you can get along personally and one with whom you can establish good professional rapport. A good source that can help you find possible contenders, as well as other professionals in the land investment business, is the Real Estate Securities and Syndication Institute, RESSI, c/o The National Association of Realtors, 925 15th Street NW, Washington, D.C. 20005.

It will also help, Arnold adds, if your group includes a good broker, real estate lawyer, and financial man like a banker or accountant. None is necessarily essential, but each is recommended for his professional understanding of the various trees and shadows in the woods that you'll be traveling through especially the first time. Such experts, in other words, expand the group's ability to size up an investment and then buy it at good terms.

Some, the lawyer, for example, could handle the legal work for the investment and be given a no-cost partial share or two for the professional services he provides. There are no standard rules for that sort of thing. They vary according to the particular situation, and sometimes they will be a little lopsided in favor of one side or the other. That's inevitable. Investing together with others of the same bent, particularly those you may know and respect, could be an excellent way to start investing in land. Instead of expending a lot of time and effort seeking good land to buy yourself, you might better direct your time and effort toward finding a good group of investors to join forces with.

Diversification

Here's another reason to team up with others to buy land. As in the stock market, it makes little sense to put all your land money in one basket. Too much is at stake, especially today as a result of the growing riskiness of land investments. Spread your chips around. Consider participating in a few promising land investments as one of a group, as well as buying land by yourself.

Three main ways to buy land

Exactly how do you go about actually buying land? What kind of papers should you sign, or not sign? What are the different ways by which land is bought and sold? What about special conditions to insist on? Common traps to avoid?

The answers can vary according to which of the three main ways to buy land you choose. They are (1) buying it outright, the do-it-yourself method; (2) the joint venture; and (3) buying into a syndication, which is usually a limited partnership agreement. Each has advantages and disadvantages.

Buying land yourself

This, the do-it-yourself route, is the simplest and easiest but not necessarily the safest and best. Making your own decisions allows you to pocket the highest potential profit because it often entails the highest risk. It's not recommended for the beginner unless it's begun in a small way.

It's chiefly for one who is seasoned and smart, or rich enough to afford good advisors and consultants to evaluate land he may buy. If you are in this category, then you need hardly concern yourself with all those boring details like local growth prospects, highest and best use, availability of utilities, drainage, and so on. Your hired advisors do it all for you in the same way they are hired all the time by big professional investors and investment bankers. If, however, you're only moderately well off, or, among other things, paying professional experts to evaluate land takes the fun out of it for you, then doing it yourself may not be a good idea.

The joint venture

This, the next step up, involves pooling your money with other people, each of whom is an equal partner in the purchase. A joint venture is generally limited to a relatively small number of people— perhaps you and a brother-in-law, another relative or two, a business associate, or a few friends. Each shares in the total risk and responsibility, as well as in the potential profit. In general, the fewer the people involved, the better a joint venture is likely to be simply because there are fewer cooks at the range.

The agreement you sign for a joint venture is crucial. Leave nothing to chance, no matter how great a group of jovial friends or relatives seem to be with you. I know, for example, of five men who formed a joint venture not too long ago to buy a tract of land for $40,000, and five years later they were offered a stunning $250,000 for the land!

That was great, except that one of the five had died and a relative inherited his share. The other four heartily approved acceptance of the offer, but the relative, an equal partner, stubbornly opposed it. He figured the land was worth at least $300,000 and should not be sold for a penny less. The joint-venture papers called for unanimous agreement among all partners before the land could be sold, so the offer could not be accepted. The relative did not relent, and at last report the group still owned the land, still paid taxes on it, and, alas, had seen it decline in value.

That's one of various perils to avoid when land is bought together with others. It can be avoided simply by having such decisions made by a majority of the partners, not by unanimity. Or the most experienced member of the group, the leader, is given decision-making authority. The contract conditions for a joint-venture agreement should be framed by an expert.

The limited partnership syndication

A syndication is defined as "an association authorized to undertake some business" or "an association of people who combine to carry out a commercial or industrial project." This, the third main way to buy land is, of course, also employed to buy other kinds of real estate.

It's organized by a promoter, or sponsor, who becomes the

majordomo, or general partner. He usually initiates the syndicate and runs it, sometimes for the management fee he will earn, sometimes for the no-cost shares in the investment he will receive for organizing the deal, or both. He goes out and sells shares in the syndication to investors, each of whom becomes a limited partner. The responsibility of each limited partner is limited to the money he invests in it. Any additional loss that may result is the responsibility of the general partner. In short, a syndicated land purchase lets you participate in the potential profit according to the number of shares you own but your liability is limited. In addition to buying land, syndications are formed to buy citrus groves, cattle ranches, and tennis court clubs (one of the recent fads) as well as brick and mortar real estate.

You can often buy into a syndication for as little as a few thousand dollars per share, or "unit." The exact price will depend, of course, on the price of the property being bought plus the legal and other costs to buy it, divided by the total number of shares sold. In one of the biggest syndications of all time, New York's Empire State Building was bought some fifteen years ago by a syndicate for $50 million, but the purchase was by no means limited to the very rich. Shares in it were priced at $10,000 a unit (so you only had to be medium rich).

That twenty-acre Chicago farm mentioned earlier that sold for $10,000 an acre was bought by a limited partnership syndicate set up with a total of nineteen units sold to investors at $2,600 a unit. That provided money for the down payment plus other purchase costs, such as the property-tax bill for the first year of ownership. The rest of the purchase price was financed. That illustrates how a land syndication's partners must make additional annual payments for carrying costs, such as interest charges and property taxes, as they come due. You are spared additional annual ownership costs if you invest in land that pays its own way, for example, income from a farm crop, or from grazing or timber rights.

Two kinds of limited partnership syndications

One of the first things to determine when offered shares in a limited partnership syndication is if it is a private or public offering. The number of investors involved generally determines whether a syndication will legally be a private or public one. This depends on your state law plus the U.S. Securities and Exchange Commission (SEC) rules. A private syndication usually has no more than about twenty-five to thirty-five investors. The exact maximum number permitted to keep it private can vary from state to state. Usually the sponsor will say that his syndicate is intended to be either a public or private one.

A private one is generally good for buying land that is not too big and highly expensive. Because it need not be registered with the SEC, that at one swoop eliminates much red tape and considerable legal and other fees that are required for a public offering. Those costs rear up because a public syndication must, like a public stock offering, be registered with the SEC. This can take a large bite out of the total potential profit, leaving a shrunken net profit for each shareholder.

On the other hand, a private syndication need not conform to the stiff rules laid down by the SEC to protect investors. The sponsor need not make "full disclosure" about all its pertinent facts, and therefore the door may be open for some shifty sleight of hand by a crooked sponsor (though he may strike you as an honest person). One sponsor of a private land syndication never mentioned, for example, that he secretly owned the land. He was syndicating it in order to unload it at a high price to unspecting investors; that is, to those buying into the syndication.

Two other tricks may be employed by slick promoters. One is the real estate broker-sponsor and general partner who rigs the deal so he will earn a 10-percent broker's fee, paid when the land is purchased, and later another 10-percent fee when it is sold. He may, in fact, be syndicating the land chiefly for this round trip commission he'll earn. Another is the sponsor who loads the deal with exorbitant up-front management fees to be paid to him before any profits can be distributed. In one such case, the promoter lined his pockets with an outrageous 60 percent of the total sales price of the land syndicated, which left very little for the unsuspecting people who had invested in his deal.

That's not to denigrate all private syndications. Many, if not most, are honest and aboveboard. But, again, you must to check on the one you may invest in, including a mandatory checking on the sponsor's integrity. Because no big brother SEC watchdog is keeping tabs on the deal, the extra risk demands careful investigation before you write out your check.

The public syndication

A public offering is generally made for a comparatively large investment. It is usually sponsored by a relatively large operator, like a Wall Street broker firm, even though his address may be in Chicago, or in Century City, Los Angeles, if not New York. Again the sponsor is the key to its likely success. SEC law requires "full disclosure" in his prospectus, which must, as we've noted, be registered with the SEC. But also as mentioned above, you pay a price for this watchdog protection. The cost of a land syndication registration with the SEC, plus legal fees and other costs can easily run from $50,000 to $100,-000, if not more. Naturally that and other costs are paid in one way or another by the investor (you).

To sum up: investing in a private land syndication with a relatively small group of others generally requires the smaller entrance fee and can be an excellent way to invest, especially in local land. It offers the high profit potential, but also high risk. A public syndication offers greater safeguards against fraud. It's usually the method employed to buy a big hunk of land at a comparatively large sum. But the profit potential per dollar invested will generally be less than that of a private syndication.

In either case, the sponsor or promoter, or general partner, whatever you call him, is the key to success or failure (also called money down the drain). His talent and integrity determine more than anything else the quality of the investment and its future promise, as well as how much of a fair shake you will get. As in nearly all other life pursuits, the person running the show determines how well the show will run.

Incidentally, don't close your mind to investing in any land syndicate just because of sour things you may have heard about some of them. Some have received notoriety, though many successful syndications have paid off good profits. Some real estate syndications sponsored by Wall Street brokerage firms during the late 1960s and early 1970s, for example, turned sour. The odor they produced and spread has hurt all syndications. And some high-powered promoters of questionable land syndications, notably in California, also left bad news and wounded investors in their wake.

The Wall Street syndicates were sponsored, by the way, by broker firms not just in New York but in other cities, too. The core of their problem was, by and large, sponsorship by unseasoned stock market broker firms rushing in to make a buck where wise men demurred. They knew no more about real estate than a lot of Dutch brokers knew about tulips some three hundred years before. They launched a spate of real estate investment syndicates involving, not so much raw land, but brick-and-mortar real estate that requires knowledge and experience about such things as operating and maintaining a big office building, or an apartment house and how to get and keep tenants.

Many broker-sponsors of these syndications lacked such knowledge and apparently also lacked the brains to hire real estate experts to operate the real estate they had bought and syndicated. Thus the painful red ink that resulted, and, alas, many investors taken to the cleaners.

By comparison, a syndication formed to invest in raw land requires virtually no buildings to manage and no unpredictable tenants to keep happy, not to mention the continual work of finding tenants and keeping the building full. That makes an investment in raw land a picnic by comparison, and the most unfettered and least complicated of all syndications.

Tax shelter benefits

How much of an income tax break can you expect by investing in a land syndication or from any other kind of investment in raw land? Not much any more, other than the routine expense deductions such as operating costs and financing charges. Unlike investing in brick-and-mortar real estate, which offers income tax deductions for such things as a building's annual depreciation, raw land doesn't depreciate. And it no longer offers the munificent tax shelter break that it formerly held out, particularly for high-income tax bracket investors. Today a land investment must stand on its own feet, but there's nothing wrong with that.

And whether you choose the joint venture or public or private syndicated-investment route, don't be lulled into the lazy's man syndrome. That holds that a firsthand view of the land and other checks on it are an unnecessary bore. Not at all. They can be just as vital as they are for a do-it-yourself investment in land. As a matter of fact, great surprises, both good or bad, can await the rare investor in syndication who actually will take it on himself to ride out and see this supposedly sparkling land so beautifully described by the promoter-sponsor. It can be a revelation well worth the time. Compare, for example, the bloodless black-print prospectus description of a property and the promoter's glowing description of it with what you see and what you may be told about the tract by local brokers or neighbors. Take a camera along to record your views of the place. That, in addition to gleaning a few other insights, usually obtainable only by a personal visit, will lift you up to the high, rarified level of one in a thousand investors. It could give you a head start leagues beyond the great majority of investors (sometimes called sheep) each of whom will barely rise from his seat to check a deal.

chapter 13

HOW TO INVEST
IN COUNTRY PROPERTY

A man whom I'll call Frank Parkin bought twenty acres of land for $4,000 in a sleepy country area. A few years later the area experienced a boom in popularity. Ten years later, as this is written, Frank's land has spiraled up in value, and a developer has offered him $100,000 for it!

The developer plans to subdivide the property and sell off two-acre plots from it for $15,000 apiece. At last report, however, Frank has not sold to the developer. He was weighing the pros and cons of subdividing the property himself. That would increase his total take from the land up to $150,000. In either case, he can't lose.

Not everyone, however, fares as well as he out in the country. There is, for example, the New York magazine editor, well known in literary circles, who was captivated by a country cottage way up on a hill in the Catskill Mountains. He bought it without a second thought. He then discovered that the old well on the place had gone dry years ago. If he and his wife wanted water for the house, a well digger would have to drill down about 600 feet at $8 per foot, but even then hitting water was not guaranteed.

Another owner was on the verge of selling some fifty acres of land to a developer for close to $200,000. That would mean a handsome profit, just what the doctor ordered for land he had bought very cheaply fifteen years earlier. But at the last minute the deal fell through because the soil was too hard and impervious. It would not pass tough new public health requirements for the septic tank systems needed for new houses built there. His land, in technical phraseology, flunked its percolation tests. Naturally the developer backed out. At last report there was little that could be done. (In the future there's a possibility that a new household waste disposal system, the "aerobic" unit, could solve the problem. It often can work well on land where a septic-tank system will not work. It is described later.)

How do you find good country land that will increase in value? How do you avoid the pitfalls? Suppose you want land only for a

Land and its soil characteristics in the country vary considerably. Land in the foreground, used for farming, buildings and roads has Class II soil, the second best of all soil types. The high slopes in the background are Class VI soil with severe limitations for most uses. (*U.S.D.A.* Photograph.)

vacation place or retirement home, should you buy a little extra to sell later at a profit? Then you could keep the rest for yourself at little or no cost. That's the wish of most people who shop for country land. What should they know? To answer those and other such questions, let's start at the beginning.

Rent before you buy

This is the best way to learn about a country area, the land available and vital facts to know before you plunge into buying. You may already know the area as a result of spending vacations there. That's fine, but don't assume too much. Sit back and look at the place from the buying point of view, that of a potential property owner and investor. If you invest, the cost of renting now could be at least partially tax deductible from your income tax. That's provided that you truly spend time shopping for a good land investment and don't try to palm off a vacation as a business expense because you spent an hour looking at a farm for sale.

Use a good local broker

Probably the second important step in our game plan for buying country property is to use a good local real estate broker. Emphasis on the words "good" and "local." He can be indispensible when you venture out in the country, also called no-man's-land.

A good broker can lead you to good land for sale you would otherwise miss and be helpful in other ways. A broker, to be sure, will not necessarily point out defects of land for sale, because he has a vested interest in it. Sometimes, though, he will surprise you and make a few disclosures that you might never guess. For one thing, a well-established broker in a community has to live with people who buy and move into the area. Some day later he might be called to sell the same property. For another, land, like humans, is seldom perfect. Besides, its warts pointed out to you may be less frightening than you may think at first. Or should they turn you off questionable land, the broker could have other, good land for you.

You can obtain the names of brokers to see in a country area in the same way you seek out brokers elsewhere. Watch the real estate ads for brokers who list land. Ask a local banker or two and other local businessmen for the names of the better brokers. Give preference to a broker who is also a realtor. But also remember that there are fewer realtors in the country than in the city, and a good nonrealtor broker can be just as reliable as a realtor. (Also see chapter 8.)

You may use a broker and also keep your eyes open for good land being sold with no broker middleman. That's done, as mentioned earlier, because the owner wants to save the broker's sales commission. Nothing wrong with that if you don't fall prey to the common buyer tendency of dealing with such a seller by yourself. You should still call in a good lawyer and any other experts recommended, however much the seller says there's no need for them and that you might as well save the money.

Where to shop

For a country place of your own, draw a circle on a map around your home with a radius of 250 miles. Shop within the circle, for that's just about the maximum distance people will travel to a place in the country. During the energy crisis the rule was amended to one tankful of gas away. It will generally give roughly the same maximum radius from home. It works out to a maximum of about four hours from home, assuming a good highway.

Prime land for country investment will generally fall within a smaller ninety-mile radius of a metropolitan center. That's the magic circle, the outer limit preferred by most people, but it's generally limited to well-off people who can afford the premium prices for land that close to home. That works out to roughly one-and-a-half hours maximum travel time from home.

If you're looking for investment land and will not live there, too, draw the same two circles—radius of 90 and 250 miles—around the center of the country area chosen. At least one metropolitan area should fall within the large circle, and preferably within the smaller circle, too.

Future growth prospects

Obviously, a good investment in country land calls for an area that will grow greatly in the future. To begin with, land prices have already soared sky-high in many a fashionable resort area. The high-priced land in many such places is also likely to continue to climb in value, but the percentage increase in its future value will not be all that great. It's often better to look for other, less popular, lower-priced areas that have not yet entered the phase of sharpest land-value increases. The entrance price for land in these more bucolic places today can be considerably less, and the potential profit percentage considerably more.

The future growth prospects of a country area is determined in much the same way as the potential growth of any area is determined as described in chapters 2 and 3. Check with the nearest planning department, the regional plan association dealing with the areas, the U.S. Department of Commerce for its data, and so on. By definition, however, SMSA data is unavailable for most country areas.

What about the accessibility of the area to and from the outer world? Is there good intra-area transportation? The high importance of a good expressway within the area is underscored by the Richard Irwin study described in chapter 4. It dramatically showed how, during the 1960s, the growth of country areas in the United States was much greater for counties with an expressway, plus a reasonably large city, than for other counties with no expressway. This is underscored by the findings from his study set forth in Table 13A.

If no major highway or expressway presently serves the area, is one planned or under construction? Check with the state and local

Table 13–A   How U.S. population grew in country areas 1960 to 1970

Total U.S. population growth for decade	13%
Total growth in metropolitan areas	17%
Nonmetropolitan areas:	
Total Growth	7%
With large city, 25,000 to 50,000 people	
With freeway, Group 1	14%
No freeway, Group 2	8%
With small city (7,500 to 25,000)	
No freeway, Group 3	11%
No freeway, Group 4	6%
Without city over 7,500	
With freeway, Group 5	8%
No freeway Group, 6	1%

Source: "Nonmetropolitan Population Change: 1960–1970," by Richard Irwin, U.S. Bureau of the Census, presented at the 1971 annual meeting of the Population Association of America, Washington, D.C.

highway departments. If a major highway neither exists nor is planned, the odds in favor of a good investment are considerably lessened, particularly if there is no reasonably large city, as shown by Irwin's figures above. He stresses, however, that his study is by no means infallible, and it may not conform to all the strict requirements ordinarily set forth for a definitive work. Nonetheless, his findings make sense, and it is the only study I know of on the subject.

How much land?

This will depend, of course, on what you can spend and again on your prime motive for buying, investment or living on the land. In either case, land, like beef, fish, and eggs, is cheaper by the dozen, as shown by Table 13B. These prices happen to be for land in Sullivan County, New York, some seventy-five miles northwest of New York City. Prices for comparable land elsewhere in the nation could be more or less. But how the price per acre declines as land size increases is much the same everywhere. The more land bought, the lower its unit price.

Moreover, finding a small parcel of good land can be especially difficult in some areas. A Bucks County, Pennsylvania, realtor says, for example, "Every man's dream is two, five, or ten acres of country property, but that doesn't exist, especially around New York. As soon as these 'chips' come on the market, they're gobbled up." The farther away from a major metropolitan center you seek land, however, the more likely a desirable small tract will be available.

Bucks County, Pennsylvania, is some seventy-five miles southwest of Times Square and, among other things, it's the setting of Kaufman and Hart's hit comedy of 1940, *George Washington Slept Here*. It was written after the authors learned about country property by buying places there, and they themselves, had slept many a night there. Read it, not only for a sustained laugh, but also to see how common pitfalls are almost timeless. Those to avoid today are many of the same as those that plagued the buyers of yesteryear.

To obtain land for yourself plus an investment profit, shop for a parcel of at least ten to twenty acres, assuming you can afford it. Carve out the portion you wish to keep and sell the rest. That's everyone's wish, and it can work out well in your favor. You end up

Table 13–B   Land Values in a Typical Country   Area in Early 1974*

Acres	Fair to Excellent Land Price Per Acre
1 to 3 acres	$2,000 to $5,000
4 to 10 acres	$1,000 to $2,000
11 to 20 acres	$ 700 to $2,500
20 to 40 acres	$ 600 to $2,000
40 to 60 acres	$ 500 to $2,000
60 to 150 acres	$ 500 to $1,500
150 to 400 acres	$ 500 to $1,500

*Reprinted with permission from the newsletter, *Country Property News.* Data source: Sullivan County Realty Company, Livingston Manor, New York. These prices do not necessarily apply to land elsewhere and they could change in the future.

with your own land free and clear, and drive off to the bank with a bag of profit on the rest.

Subdividing land

One rule of thumb holds that you should buy three times the acreage you want for yourself, but the whole tract should be usable with little waste. You keep roughly one-third for yourself, and divide the rest into two separate parcels for sale. Presto! You have produced the smaller, highly desirable tracts that are often so scarce and are sold the moment they hit the market.

It may not always work out that easy way, and besides, subdividing is not done overnight. Should you decide to do it, you'll have bills coming in for surveys, engineering costs, and possibly some new legal problems. A new road or two may have to be put in—who pays for this? And the taxes on each of the subdivided plots, including yours, will almost certainly go up.

There's also a limit to the number of subdivided lots allowed before the Internal Revenue Service calls you a professional real estate developer, which means higher taxes. Among other things, you could lose your favored amateur's right to a capital gains tax on the profit from subdivided land sold off. Your profit is then considered ordinary income. You can avoid that pitfall by remaining a small-scale subdivider. Don't give in to the temptation of making a killing by buying many acres and selling lots galore from them. Current tax law, as this is written, ordinarily puts you in the professional subdivider's class when you sell five or more subdivided lots in a year. But the law could change. So before plunging into the subdividing game, check the tax ramifications.

If you subdivide, you might not consider it very neighborly if one of your land buyers turns his plot next door into a chicken farm or mobile home park. This has happened, alas, and will continue to happen to the nicest people. You can avoid it, by putting a sharp hook and small-print restriction in your sales contract. The contract could read, for example, that no other use (besides a house or two) will be permitted without your written permission. Have a good lawyer take care of that, as well as combing the contract for other protection you may need.

chapter 14

BUYING A PLACE IN THE COUNTRY FOR YOURSELF

This chapter is primarily for the reader who is concerned, not so much in country property as an investment, but chiefly in property to live on. It may or may not have a house to start with. And possibly you might consider a little more land than necessary with the idea that later you will sell off some of it for a profit. But that's a secondary consideration. The main goal is to obtain a really good place for its living pleasure for you and your family. Other readers interested more in country property for investment might skip through this chapter.

What's the smallest, least costly amount of land you might buy that will be satisfactory and insure privacy? Privacy is the key. A small, relatively inexpensive tract of land can sometimes offer greater privacy to its occupants than a great expanse at far greater cost.

Privacy depends first on topography. A desert island surrounded by shark waters can represent extreme privacy (if nothing else). Similarly, land bounded at least in part by a river or lake, a steep hill or mountain, public parkland, or other such restricted land will at once be a big step in the right direction for your future privacy. In other words, what might be built on the land next to you

151

to threaten your privacy? It depends largely on what *can* or cannot be built there.

The local zoning is the second controlling factor on privacy and what is likely to be built on the land nearby. What's the likelihood of a gas station or fast-food restaurant, or both, being built there in the future? Having such nearby companions in the future can hinge on the zoning, assuming the land itself is suitable. Local officials can tell you what the zoning is, but be forewarned. Many rural communities lack zoning laws, and even where they exist their protection for you depends on strict enforcement. Are they enforced? Or will officials bend to heavy pressure (often from local property owners who want to sell at top prices) and let the zoning be torpedoed?

The two requirements for privacy

These are freedom from visual and audio intrusion. Both can be achieved by buying a very large tract for yourself with plenty of land and trees on all sides. You isolate yourself in the middle of it where nobody can see or hear you, and vice versa. Fine, if you have the money and can find the tract with the right isolation-booth qualifications.

Otherwise you may have no choice but to choose marginal land in the sense that it may seem denuded and lacking in privacy. Don't despair, however. Privacy can often be achieved, even on quite small sites, by imaginative landscaping or clever architectural design. You simply cut off outsiders' views of you for visual privacy, and cut off noise from the outer world for audio privacy. Then you will feel totally comfortable, and you will be private in your house and home. A big stride toward each can be realized by good architectural design of the house you build on the land. Exterior measures can also help greatly, and knowing about them can help when you shop for land.

Visual privacy is generally easier to attain. It often can be had merely by erecting a visual barrier—a row of fir trees, hemlocks, high hedges, or even a wooden fence—between you and outsiders. It's amazing how such a simple change can transform the property behind it.

Striving for audio privacy is what sends many people fleeing to a large, isolated country site miles from everyone else. But buying a great big tract of land just to guarantee privacy from neighbors on all sides is often silly, unless you're driven up the wall every time a neighbor sneezes. Quiet, serene surroundings, to be sure, require land where you can enjoy the birds and the bees and not be battered by the roar from a nearby jetport or a local factory. To avoid such pounding, check for such noises at a site you may buy with your own ears. You would also do well to be sure that no new superhighway or jetport is planned within audio distance. (That is unless, of course, such new development is desired so the value of your land will rise.)

But just as land can be under water in April but Sahara dry in August, it can also be quiet as a church in summer but noisy like a circus in winter. That may be all right for a summer place, but not desirable for a year-round house. Heavy foliage with all the trees in bloom plus a favorable wind could insulate you from noise in summer, but a 180-degree change in that summer protection could let a noise thunder in come winter. If there is big noisemaker nearby, an honest neighbor or two might tell you how much of a nuisance it is in winter. Or you might put off the purchase until you can check the place yourself come winter.

Mass is beautiful

Noise infringing on a house often can be suppressed by literally stonewalling it, in the words of a former U.S. president. A brick or stone wall built between you and the noise source could stop the noise waves. The thicker the wall and the greater its mass, the better. The wall should go as close as possible to the noise source. To subdue bothersome traffic noise, for example, put the wall right along the street, if possible, between the traffic and you.

This was done by a family I know with a waterfront property located on the west bank of a lovely portion of the Hudson River in upstate New York. A local street borders the back of the property and on it monster buses go by twice an hour. They built a brick wall to close off the rear of their terrace, and it achieved quiet wonders. The buses still go rumbling by but the wall sharply reduces their noise level just a few yards away on the other side of the wall inside the terrace. The wall is attractive too, and also serves as a visual barrier.

A thick row of trees can also insulate you from noise, provided they are practically jungle-thick. To obtain the same insulation from noise as that provided by a twelve-inch brick or stone wall, you would need a small forest of trees in full leaf at least thirty feet deep. A writer I know applied this knowledge in self-defense. He was on the verge of selling his country home because of the noise from people cavorting every day in the swimming pool next door. A row of trees stood between his house and the pool, but he still could not concentrate and write with all that noise. Then he put up a brick wall on his property line between the pool and his house to insulate him from the pool racket. It works just fine. The mass of the wall bounces back the noise waves sufficiently to preserve his sanity and let him work. It also saved the property for his family and himself after he almost sold it.

I've gone into a little detail about achieving sight and sound privacy because it can be helpful when you shop for country property. Achieving each are prime motives for buying country property, though few people realize it in these terms. Know how to judge land for such privacy or how each can be achieved with a little ingenuity, and it can make an enormous difference, as well as contribute to your future sanity.

How to check country property

Use the buying checklist in chapter 17, which is recommended for all land. But because country property can hold special surprises for you, here are special things to know about it.

Accessibility. How close is it to the nearest country store? The nearest town or village? Don't overlook practical things like these even if you want the most remote location. It's no fun to travel thirty miles for a Sunday paper or a quart of milk (or whatever your liquid). Even if you're buying land as an investment with no intention of living there, its future value could still be downgraded because it is too inaccessible.

Beside adequate road frontage, what about the cost of a driveway into the property? A long, winding driveway, if one is required to get to the heart of the property, can cost a fortune. So determine in advance how close to the road a house can be built.

Water. Even if there's a well on the property don't take it for granted. Have the water tested for chemical purity and flow during the dry season. If there's no well, you'll have to drill one. This "is often the most expensive thing to determine in evaluating a country lot," says geologist Eugene Bourdreau, author of the excellent book *Buying Country Land* (Macmillan; $4.95).

Don't be shy. Follow the customary practice of making the purchase of land depend on adequate water being found within a reasonable depth (say 200 feet) from the surface. You may have to pay to drill a well—at $5 to $10 per foot, sometimes more—before the land is yours, and should water not be found, you're out that much money. But this is plainly preferable to paying the full price and then learning that water is unobtainable except at prohibitive cost.

Talk to drillers. Get the paid opinion beforehand of a good local geologist about water availability on the land. Consult local government experts such as the county agent, town engineer, and public health department people. Once you strike water, have it chemically tested to be sure it's drinkable, and make sure there is a sufficient water flow for your family.

Utilities. Electricity and a telephone are generally essential. The local electric and telephone companies can bring lines into almost any house but they will sometimes charge you and the cost could be high. It depends on the distance to be spanned from their nearest lines. Get a firm estimate of the cost from each.

Household waste disposal. That's the euphemism for sewage disposal when you live beyond the city sewer line, which, of course, is where most country houses are. It's not the world's most engaging subject but it's nonetheless crucial. Without approved sewage disposal for the land, no house or any other construction will be allowed.

The most common disposal method is the septic tank, provided one will work on your soil. This is determined by that "percolation test." Holes are dug in the ground, filled with water and the time required for the water to settle and be absorbed is clocked. A percolation rate of no more than about twenty minutes is most desirable. A rate of more than an hour will generally rule out a septic tank. Talk to the local public health department about this. Have a percolation test of the soil taken prior to buying land, or make your purchase conditional on satisfactory waste disposal (as well as water supply).

If a septic tank will not work, consider an "aerobic" waste disposal unit. Ask local officials about its acceptability locally. The aerobic disposal unit, a recent innovation for houses, is considerably better and more efficient than a septic tank. It's as great an advance over the septic tank as the flush toilet was over the backyard out-house. It can be a godsend in an area where septic tanks are of questionable value. The names of recommended brands and their manufacturers' addresses can be had by writing to the National Sanitation Foundation, 3475 Plymouth Road, Ann Arbor, Michigan 48105. Include a stamped, self-addressed envelope. Because it is new, however, the aerobic unit is still not approved for use in all areas.

Orientation. This has to do with how a house is situated on the land and its exposures to the sun, wind, and view. It's far more important than many people realize for a well-designed house. Also now with the energy crisis, a house with really good orientation to the sun and wind can be heated in winter and air-conditioned in summer for as much as 40 percent less energy than a house with poor orientation. So when you look at land, visualize how a house can be built and situated on it. You can make yourself conscious of the power of orientation and its various exposures by examining the house you now live in.

The ideal site for a house is on high land with a good, if not panoramic, view to the south (and preferably, of course, with a pastoral stream winding through the property). In other words, the very best orientation for a house is broadside to the south. All other things equal, the house should be designed and built with its main living areas and largest glass areas opened up full to the bright south, and conversely its back turned to the grey north.

A house opened up full to the south is easiest to keep cool in summer and easiest to heat in winter. It's easiest to cool because windows on the south are easiest to shade from the high overhead summer sun blasting down in July and August. They're easily shaded by wide roof overhangs designed into the house over south windows, or by other comparable window-shading devices. At the same time few windows are left exposed to the hot morning sun from the east —yes, from the hot east—and the scorching afternoon sun from the west.

Then in winter, the very same large windows and main parts of your house on the south will let the winter sun, now coming in from much lower in the sky, pour welcome sunshine and brightness into the heart of your house. On sunny days you'll hardly need any additional heat from the furnace. That's especially when you have turned the back of your house to the cold north winds.

Now, of course, not every house need be oriented to the south for maximum benefits. A year-round house in a warm southern climate could face north, turning its back on the hot sun from the south. And it need not worry about cold north winds in winter. A vacation house in the North used mainly in summer also could be oriented to the north for summer coolness, or beneficially even to the east or the west, depending on the site. And a great view in another direction may be too good to pass up when a house is designed and built. Something else has to give and it may have to be aspects of orientation that must suffer.

The best southern orientation of house and home is, in general, obtained on land that is located on the south side of the road. Then the house on it can face to the private south side of the property for privacy, and turn its back to the public road in front as well as to the cold north winds in winter. Next best site is generally land on the north side of the road.

Not every site will meet those starting needs, of course. But no matter what the exposure characteristics of a tract of land and where the road in front may be, a good house can still be put on it with good orientation. Sometimes the house can be turned to the south, no matter where the road in front may be. That may take careful design by a good architect and how it's done depends on the land. It's generally best, however, to avoid a site that limits your house to facing either due east or west. However spectacular it is, a west view in summer can be hell because it looks right into the hot afternoon sun. Sometimes this can be handled reasonably efficiently as it has been done in some—but decidedly not all—houses atop the Pacific Palisades in California overlooking the ocean to the west.

As a matter of fact, call in an architect to check land before you buy. Yes, still another expert added to your list of paid consultants. Just set aside a lump sum of $1,500, say, for all such advice, and consider it a cheap price to pay for insurance. But like paying a doctor for preventive medicine, his fee also could be saved later many times over as a result of his precautions and advice. He can tell you about the land's suitability for a house, how it lends itself to good orientation and proper siting and about such things as sewage disposal and entrance road. In all, he can be a boon in helping you choose good land. You might also consider, when you build, one of the better prefabricated houses on the market. Even then a good architect can still be of much help, if only in siting the house and adapting it to the land.

Buying the land with an old house on it

I'm going to be short and sweet on this topic. Almost every old house for sale will be in need of some repairs and modernization. Often that's why it's being sold. But for some reason the old house in the country always seems to be twice as full of problems, though they're not always readily apparent. There are about a dozen or so things in a used house that are likely to be run-down and in need of repairs or modernization. Not every one of them is necessarily defective in every used house, especially if the last owner has maintained the place well.

These most common causes of trouble in the typical used house include an old-fashioned kitchen and bathroom (which you may or may not be able to live with), run-down plumbing (which you cannot live without when it goes); dangerously ancient wiring, senile furnace and heating system, termites or rotted structural underpinnings, worn-out roofing, and exterior walls and windows in need of a new paint job.

Some of these potentially expensive troubles can be easily spotted; others may be harder to find. To check on all, call in a house inspection engineer or a local builder or contractor to check the house. He'll take about $100 to $150, more or less, of that insurance fund you set aside. Also get estimates of the total cost of repairs and modernization. You may decide to tackle the work yourself, which is fine if you can manage it. But don't bite off more than you can chew.

A few final tips

Shop for land with a waterfront. The most desirable land will always be land on a lake, river, or ocean, or with its own pond or stream. It can be expensive, to be sure, but if you can swing it, by all means do. Living there will by itself pay off in great personal pleasure. Should you sell all or part of it, you will get the highest price. And during an economic slump, the high desirability of land with water helps its sales appeal when other land goes begging.

Water can sometimes be deceptive, however. For example, don't mistake a swamp for a lake, and don't be carried away by a soft-bottom pond. An old timer can quickly tell you if it's a genuine body of water. He'll tell you, for example, how a soft-bottom pond can develop a case of hydrosulphide which has an odor unrelated to perfume. A pond should have a permanent hard bottom; a full-fledged lake is even better.

Put your priorities in order. What's your primary wish? Do you most want land on which to live? Or land that will turn a profit for you? Nearly everyone wants both, but the inability to decide which is more important tends to blur things and hinder a successful quest for one or both. Clearly establish which is more important, and it will be easier to find good land that will meet that preferred desire—and it will often meet the other desire, as well.

Don't buy prematurely. This is mainly for the investor. Country land tends to go through a longer undeveloped phase, and a more extended predeveloped stage than land in city and suburban areas where growth patterns develop more swiftly. That's partly because of the more relaxed pace of things in the country, because country population growth is slower and there's more land around for fewer buyers than in city or suburb.

Take a camera with you when you shop for land. Take pictures, not necessarily for the record, but to jog your memory later when you mull over a piece of land. They can also remind you about a tract that you had just about decided against. But now in comparison with other land you've since seen it assumes new desirability.

Get what you pay for. The exact size, corner to corner, of country property is not always spelled out clearly or even known for sure. Country records are more casual and informal than city records. A boundary description may contain archaic terms like "rods, chains, or perches." A corner of the property deeded to a son long ago may be located at an oak stump that has vanished, yet the deed still has it for a boundary point. Other uncertainties coupled with no accurate survey also can mean that land sold as "approximately ten acres" could turn out later to be actually seven acres, or possibly twelve. That happens.

To protect against being shortchanged on acreage, the contract should include a safety clause like this: "Should the property prove by survey or other good measure to be substantially smaller or larger than stated, the purchase price will be adjusted proportionately." If you don't want more land, then you should have the right to return any excess. If you have been shortchanged, you deserve a refund. If, however, the seller has left for parts unknown, you are left holding the bag. That possibility can be avoided if you are financing the purchase and still owe money on the land; the money owed is reduced accordingly. Or you can withhold a portion of the purchase price until the land can be accurately measured.

chapter 15

BUYING LOTS FROM
A LAND DEVELOPMENT
COMPANY

There are more than ten thousand land development companies in the United States that sell lots to the public. Some are giant corporations such as McCulloch Oil, IT&T, and the Deltona Corporation, though size and well-known names are not necessarily guarantees of reliability. Most are little known except within the region where they're located.

Most sell subdivided lots in resort areas throughout the country, or in retirement communities chiefly in the South (mostly in Florida) and the Southwest. The lots are sold for as little as $50 down and $50 to $100 a month for about ten years.

According to surveys of buyers, the great majority of people who buy this land—more than 60 percent—buy not just for the land and a house later, but primarily because "It's a good investment." The typical land salesman pushes hard at this motive. He'll say, "Here's your chance to get a piece of the action. Buy now, and in a few years you can sell at a big profit!"

Yet buying land from any one of these developers ranks at the very bottom of all real estate in terms of its investment caliber. In a very few select cases, the purchase of such land might give you a modest profit, assuming you can sell it. Often you cannot sell for at least ten years and sometimes not even then.

161

The high price of sales and development

Such land sometimes can be a good thing *if* you plan to have a house built on it and live there some day. As an investment, however, it shapes up poorly simply because of its basic economics. The actual value of the raw land you are buying often comes to as little as 15 percent of the sales price you pay to buy it, according to S. H. Wills, Chairman and President of GAC Corporation, Miami, Florida, one of the largest national land development companies.

That's because, Wills frankly says, the rest of the purchase price you pay must go for your share of the new roads, utility lines, and everything else that is needed to turn each subdivision into a living, breathing community. Other portions of your price are earmarked for advertising and sales costs, and the developer's overhead and

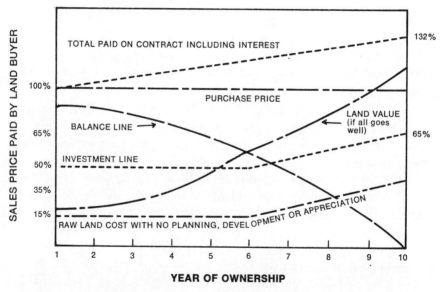

The actual cost of the raw land bought from a land sales company can run only 15 percent of the sales price paid for the land, as shown here. The value of the land bought will generally take at least nine to ten years to appreciate to the sales price paid. These figures from the GAC Corporation are estimates based on a normal installment contract for land bought with a 10 percent down payment in cash and the balance financed for ten years with 7 percent interest paid on the declining balance.

profit, as shown in the accompanying chart from Mr. Wills.

There's also the rule of fifths, a rule of thumb many developers use when they buy land. They figure that one-fifth of the sales price paid them for a lot (excluding the house on it) will go for the raw land cost; one-fifth for improvements (utilities, roads, engineering); one-fifth for interest charges, carrying costs and miscellaneous; and two-fifths for advertising, sales, administrative costs, and profit.

The developer therefore must jack up the retail sales price of each developed lot he sells to at least five times the cost to him of the raw land itself. His other costs may rise even more, especially if high-powered (thus high-cost) advertising and sales promotion are needed, and that can swell his budget. The usual result is that the raw land portion of his land sales price goes down to 15 percent or less of the price he must charge for each lot.

The subdivided lot sold to the public will be worth little more until later after the company develops all the land and turns it into a live community. That calls for the roads, utility lines, and other such services that must be installed. Plenty of individual lots must be sold, houses built on the lots, and people must move in. That usually takes five to ten years from the first land sale until at least a portion of the community is built up and lived in. Only then will any land in the community begin to be worth anything close to its retail sales price. That, in other words, means close to the price a buyer paid for it.

Selling early

Many a buyer figures, nonetheless, that he will sell his lot or two long before that, pocket his profit, and whatever happens to the community later is none of his business. Nice work if you can swing it, except there's usually a second trap awaiting the naive buyer who counts on a profit from a relatively fast resale. The land he's bought generally cannot be sold for ten years, if not more. That's because of a small-print restriction in the contract, or because the developer himself does not own the land. How then can he pass on the deed to it to you or anyone else?

George K. Bernstein, head of the Office of Interstate Land Sales, part of the U.S. Department of Housing and Urban Development, the government watchdog over national land sales, explains it in this way. Many such developers don't own the land they sell because they bought it on the cuff, with a mortgage, in other words. That's the way things are often done in the business. Besides, it doesn't make sense to use up all one's capital just for the land when a substantial amount of money will be required to sell the subdivided lots and develop the land. If all goes well and the lots sell, the developer will pay off his land mortgage later with money received from the people buying lots from him.

The third much-publicized problem in land sales is the presence of a number of crooks in the business. These slick operators often have little or no intention of developing the land they sell. Often their land is located way out in the middle of barren nowhere, miles from the nearest passable road. It may be snake-infested desert, or swampland, or for other reasons hopeless. Such land can be sold only because it is sold by mail, or sold by high-pressure sales teams sent into cities and suburbs. The victims who are pressured into buying it never see it, at least before buying. Often the buyer is not allowed to see it before signing for it and parting with his money.

There are also many legitimate developers selling land in new subdivisions. Buy from an honest operator and you can be reasonably well assured that you will not be defrauded. But then, too, don't expect that the land will necessarily be a good investment, per se. The honest developer will frankly tell you that. You might make a little money selling the land later, but seldom more than the same money would earn for you in the bank.

But hope springs eternal. You may still decide to buy land from a land sales company. Before you buy I suggest that you perform the following half-dozen little prepurchase acts of caution:

1. Write for the free pamphlet "Get the Facts . . . Before Buying Land," from the U.S. Department of Housing and Urban Development, Washington, D.C. 20410.

2. Write for the report "Buying Land," free from the Council of Better Business Bureaus, Inc., 1150 17th Street NW, Washington, D.C. 20036. Include a stamped self-addressed envelope.

3. Get a copy of the property report on the land. Most developers must provide this, and if not, they violate the law.

4. Read each of the above.

5. Buy only from an established land developer. That means only one who has completed at least one other successful subdivision, one that is thriving today. If he has accomplished that, the experi-

ence automatically ranks him far above 90 percent of all land developers who are doing it the first time.

6. Visit the land and see it before buying. That will automatically rank you above 90 percent of all buyers.

Good luck!

chapter 16

EIGHTEEN TIPS ON BUYING LAND

1. Diversify

Don't pin all your hopes on one piece of land any more than you would bet your lifetime savings on one stock in the stock market. It's too chancy, obviously. Spread your land money around on two or three different pieces of land at least and, if possible, land in different places not too alike. The success of each investment will not hinge on the same fortuitous circumstances all coming together at the same time. Besides, the growing risk involved in buying land increases the likelihood that even some of the very best land investments will not pan out. Or they will take considerably longer to ripen than originally seemed likely.

2. Buy when something is going to happen

Everybody knows that land gets a big boost when a new highway is to come through. It could also be a new bridge, new mass transit system, or new shopping center, industrial plant, or large government complex. Like a giant magnet, such new developments bring people and growth, and their ripples can spread some distance.

Inevitably as day follows night, there is a sharp increase in land values, though not all the land around will necessarily climb in value. And you need not buy instantly on the news of something happening. It's often better, in fact, to sit back and evaluate the situation, confirm its real portents, and then buy at one of the later best times to buy after a new happening has been announced. See chapter 5.

3. Don't look back

Don't be put off good land just because it sold in the past at a low price compared with its present price tag. That's a common mistake made by local people in an changing area where land values are on the climb. Many people, however, will never forget that the Johnson property once, long ago, could have been had for a mere $100 an acre. "And now they're asking $1,500! Outlandish!"

Well, if it's good land where much growth is still to come, its value could very well rise to $15,000 an acre! And possibly more. Look ahead, not back.

4. Don't deal with an out-of-the-area real estate broker

It's best to deal with a broker whose home base is the area in which he's showing you land, in other words, one who is established there and knows the place well. Some brokers will latch on to a listing located beyond their familiar territory. They have no qualms about selling it to anyone, despite their ignorance of the land itself and the area in which it's located.

Of course, an out-of-area broker could put you in touch with good land for sale in an area beyond his geographical scope. But then a good broker will also introduce you to a local broker in the area who can take it from there. A multiple-listing arrangement occurs in which both brokers will share the one commission, should you buy.

5. Fly over the land

Seeing land from the air can give you a unique view and special insight into an area. Do it off and on, especially after a heavy rain (to observe drainage patterns and possible flooding), and during the late afternoon rush hour to see interesting travel patterns develop, such as heavy traffic in a direction of heavy future growth.

Aerial maps, available for many areas, also can be helpful. They sometimes can be had from government agencies, or from private firms who sell them as a business. A good broker can tell you where to obtain aerial maps of his local area.

6. Don't be unduly swayed by land for sale at a low price

The price can be deceptive. Land selling for a very low price has historically been the downfall of the countless buyers who equate low price with a bargain value. It is no bargain when it continues to sell for little more than the same low price years later.

You can, as a matter of fact, today buy thousands of acres of excellent ranchland in the United States for no more than $50 to $75 an acre. There's all you could want for sale in the West and Southwest, only much of it is accessible only by airplane. To be sure, there are also all the stories about people who bought huge tracts of land dirt-cheap and sold later for a fortune in profits. Some are true, but most are fiction.

The important point is to determine what land is really worth now, and what it is likely to be worth five to ten years from now. That's fundamental. Then work backward to determine if its present price is realistic and worth paying now.

7. Don't overpay for land

This is the reverse side of the coin. It's a particular danger to avoid in a growing area where everyone and his cousin Joe says that all the land around is going sky-high tomorrow and you had better buy today because it will be too late tomorrow. That's when the "greater fool" phenomenon goes into high gear. The same land is sold repeatedly, each time at a higher price, and each time to a new buyer who figures he can sell it again shortly to some fool who will pay even more for it. The last buyer ends up holding the bag. That's the extreme form of paying too much, with land being bought and sold at prices far above genuine value.

Coming down to earth, good land often will, to be sure, sell at a price somewhat above its current market value; that's to be expected. Market value is determined by a professional appraisal.

8. Don't buy prematurely

Contrary to popular belief, land does not continually rise in value over the years. Much land, in fact, lies fallow in value as well as use, until it enters its predeveloped stage. Its value begins to climb only after the moment at which it's likely to be put to use in the foreseeable future. Buying it too long before that time can cost you dearly in taxes and other holding costs, as well as tying up capital in an asset that sometimes cannot be sold at all.

9. Be sure of the facts before you buy

Even a report in a newspaper or magazine should be checked before it influences land-buying decisions. No one but an idiot will buy land because of hearsay or rumor, however impressive the information source may seem to be. Such "facts" should be verified and confirmed at the source. Go directly to the highway department for a copy of the actual route of a planned new road, or to whomever is the source of the reported development. Sometimes, to be sure, you may be privy to confidential information from, say, an influential insider, and it could well be a sound tip.

10. Make your own little growth studies

Working with a map, note the main highways feeding in and out of the area you're interested in. Note where the principal growth has so far occurred, and the highway that goes on to the next large city. Mark on your map highways or other transportation routes being built or planned for the future, also the location of other notable developments planned. Use aerial photos and the U.S. Geological Survey maps for the degree of development in various parts of the area; also an up-to-date zoning map from the zoning board for the kind of use allowed on available land. If sewage disposal is an important consideration locally (and it is nearly all over), mark in the present city sewer lines and, in dotted lines, future sewer lines planned.

If available, obtain past aerial views of the area going back five, ten, and twenty years. Put together, they can show a dramatic picture of the past and present growth unfolding in the area. As you study the emerging pattern, some new future growth paths will unfold before your eyes. This is no exercise for the lazy man, but for another it can be fascinating diversion—and rewarding.

11. Buy when others must sell

Much land could be had at reduced prices during the Nixon tight-money recession of 1969 and 1970, and again during the next tight-money crunch a few years later. "For Sale" signs sprouted up on land all over as owners, pinched for cash, had to sell. Few buyers, how-ever, can be found at such times for the same reason—lack of liquid-ity.

A smart investor, however, prepares for just such a cyclical turn of events, and then can practically call his shots for good land at reduced prices. But you must have the cash on hand to buy, and also have your homework done on which land will offer the greatest investment potential. Being cyclical, other similar opportunities will surely come in the future after other future cycles of high prosperity, loose money, and bull markets run their course.

12. Beware of the scrambled egg-parcel

Of all things, a single parcel of land that you may buy could turn out later to be broken up into two or three separate pieces. Small odd-shaped "strips" or "gores" of foreign property could lie in the middle of your land and complicate plans to use or later sell the land. You've got scrambled-egg land.

To be certain that land you may buy is not scrambled, it should be clearly and precisely described in your contract as a single, inte-grated parcel. It's best, of course, when there's a survey, though this is not always available. You could pay for a survey, but this can get expensive. To be sure you're getting a coherent tract is particularly important when you buy adjacent property from two or more differ-ent owners. A guarantee of continuity should be obtained from each seller. Your lawyer also should be on the ball to protect you.

13. Avoid a sharp increase in property taxes when you buy land

The tax assessment and then the property tax itself often shoots up after land has been sold. That's because the sales price is higher than the previous value attached to the land, and because the sale calls attention to the land. This happens more and more because local governments are under pressure to increase their tax income in every way.

The property tax should not rise, however, when land is not bought outright and therefore no title transfer is made for a while. This is routine, of course, when the purchase is financed, and the title to the property is not transferred to you until the final payment is made. You may, however, want the right to prepay the mortgage in full at any time, should you decide to sell the land. That option should be written into the contract.

To prevent a hefty tax hike, various purchase agreements can be made depending on the circumstances. For that matter, you need not contract to buy the land, but instead pay for an option to buy it before a certain date in the future. You may exercise the option at any time up to its deadline. Or the option runs out and the land reverts to the seller. Whatever route you take, let sleeping dogs lie. Discuss it with a good lawyer, and have him arrange a legitimate purchase that does not leave you vulnerable to a sharp property tax increase after the purchase.

14. May you build on the land?

The choicest and highest value of all land today is that which comes with approval to build on it; thus, no hitches can prevent its development. Even partial approval can mean the battle half won. The soil of a country property, for example, may have passed a percolation test, which means no sewage-disposal problem. That can be a big plus.

Sometimes, however, an approval runs out within a certain time and is then no longer valid. So if a seller tells you that building approval has already been obtained, check on it. See the approval paper and be sure that it has not expired.

15. Buy the acre and sell the lot

John Jacob Astor supposedly said it first. You become a subdivider, in other words, and you could double your profits. But it's no picnic, and there's a limit to the subdividing permitted before you're considered a professional and your profits taxed as ordinary income, rather than as a capital gain, as noted in chapter 13. It's recommended only if you have the stamina and inclination for it, plus enough capital to finance the work. You'll also have to wait out inevitable delays and, among other things, wait for time-consuming approvals required for subdivision approval. It was a lot easier in Astor's time, but it can still pay.

16. Has a subdivision map been filed for land you may buy?

Find this out whether or not you plan to subdivide. If such a map has been filed, the seller should tell you and cite the relative facts in your sales contract. Is the map still valid? What about other requirements of the filing?

Even if the map is still valid, a subsequent change in local zoning could put a hitch in things. Or the prior approval might give individual buyers of the subdivided lots special rights over streets and/or parts of the tract. Such hindrances to you or any subsequent buyer could thus put a cloud over the land. And if the validity of the map has already lapsed, or will lapse shortly, the value of the property could be reduced, thereby hurting your chance to sell later, though this depends on your intentions for the land.

17. Who are your prospective neighbors?

This can usually be determined from the tax map. (It is not always possible when, for example, adjoining land is owned by a figurehead corporation to mask the real owner.) Contact prospective neighbors and let them know, if necessary, that you may buy the land nearby. What's good for them can be good for you, and vice versa. What plans, if any, does each have for his land? Or her land? Is it for sale? What will eventually happen to neighboring land could obviously have an impact on the future value of your land, so the answers are grist for your mill. Of course, some owners will be suspicious (as they are of everything) and not talk to you. But others will share their knowledge, and all can benefit.

18. Make your own checks on land you may buy

A lawyer or real estate counselor can do it for you (and bill you, of course). But it can be instructive to make your own visit to the town hall or county courthouse and check on the (1) current tax assessment, (2) annual tax bill, (3) zoning category, and such other things as the plot's title history and who the different owners have been and are today.

While there you might learn other handy information from clerks and officials having to do with real estate and land. Get the names of a key employee or two who knows things, and then you might call him later, if necessary, for an important fact. Most important, however, is that a little personal research can provide an invaluable insight into how things work in real estate and give you a deeper insight into the art of buying and selling land.

chapter 17

CHECKLIST FOR BUYING LAND

Location

1. How good are the growth prospects for the surrounding area?
2. What population growth is predicted for the area in the next ten years? Is that relatively high, medium, or low growth?
3. Is there at least one good major highway in the area? If not, is one planned or being built?
4. Are there any other good transportation facilities that will give the area a lift?
5. Is the land directly and easily accessible?
6. Does the land have ample frontage on a good road?
7. Is there public transportation within convenient walking distance?
8. What is the travel time to the central business district?

Use of the land

9. What is the highest and best potential use for the land?
10. Will it be permitted by the local zoning?
11. If desirable, is a zoning change for a different use from that permitted now likely to be approved?

175

12. Is the land well located for the best use? For example, for stores, a shopping center, or other commercial use, is the land easily accessibile to potential customers? Is there good public transportation? Is the market area large enough? Is there enough room for parking? Can all necessary utilities be provided? See chapter 10, on this point, and on 13 and 14 below.

13. If the land is to be used for housing, is it located in an area of high-income housing (thus highest land value)? Will it take high-density multiple housing (for highest land value of all)? Are the local schools good? Are there stores nearby? Churches? A park or other recreation facilities? Is the location within acceptable commuting distance to the local job centers?

14. If the land is intended for industrial use, is there ready access to a major highway? To a railroad? Will the surrounding area provide a good pool of workers?

15. Is the land topographically suitable for the use? Can it be built on without major construction problems? For example, is it dry and free of flooding?

Utilities

16. Is water easily obtainable? If water rights are required, will they come with the property?

17. Can sewage disposal be made into a city sewer line? If not, is a sewer line coming? If necessary, what alternate sewage disposal can be used for the land?

18. Can electricity be provided easily? How much will the electric company charge to provide electric service?

19. Can gas energy be provided?

20. Will a storm sewer be required? Can this be easily provided?

Aesthetics

21. Is the land visually attractive? Does its appearance increase its sales appeal?

22. Are there enough trees? If not, will new trees or other landscaping be needed? Or will some trees have to be removed? Can the land be readily seen from the road?

23. Do the adjacent properties help or hurt the value of the land? What are the adjacent properties used for? If vacant, how are these properties likely to be used?

Environmental considerations

24. Does a local or regional environmental control administration (ECA) hold jurisdiction over the land?
25. What kind of environmental controls and requirements are likely over the land use?
26. Will an environmental impact study have to be made before land-use approval? If so, what will this mean, based on other studies made for other comparable land?
27. Will a local slow-growth or no-growth law hold back use of the land? If no such law currently applies, is one being considered?

Local taxes

28. What is the tax assessment on the property? How much is it likely to rise after you buy the property?
29. What are the total annual property taxes?
30. How does the local tax rate compare with the tax rate in nearby communities? Is it favorable or unfavorable to an extent that will influence future use of the land?
31. Is the local tax rate likely to go up in the future?
32. Has the recent trend been toward higher or lower taxes locally? Have there been substantial increases in recent years? If so, will they continue?
33. What do local tax officials say about current and future tax policies?
34. Where does the bulk of the property-tax revenue come from locally? Housing? Commercial or industrial property? How will that influence the proposed use of the land? How much will the local tax policies, in other words, influence development of the land?
35. Will all taxes due have been paid on the land by the sale date?

Legal and other facts

36. Does the seller own clear title to the property?
37. Has an easement or other right to the land been given to anyone in the past? If so, how will it affect the future of the land and its use?
38. What about the size of the property and its boundary lines? Are these clearly known and established by an up-to-date survey? Or will you have to provide one?
39. Is the property a totally integrated piece of land not separated or cut up by land owned by others?
40. Are you using a good local lawyer, one really familiar with the area? Is he well practiced in real estate transactions?

The value of the land

41. What is its present market value? Has this been determined by a professional appraiser?
42. What has other comparable land sold for recently? Should this land sell for more or less?
43. What is the land likely to be worth five years from now? Ten years?
44. Is the estimate of future worth based on the value of comparable land already developed?
45. What are the best financing terms obtainable for buying the land?
46. How do they compare with customary terms being given for other land bought and sold recently?
47. Is the land really worth buying? Is it really worth buying now?
48. Is the price right?
49. Have you done your homework? Do you know all that can and should be known about the land?
50. Now, how do you genuinely *feel* about this land, this property? Is it the best land you can buy now? Or does a serious question or two remain in your mind about it? If not, and if all the facts add up in favor of buying—despite a drawback or two, which is inevitable—then the land could indeed be a good purchase!

appendix A

IS INVESTMENT IN VACANT LAND ON THE FRINGE OF METROPOLITAN AREAS A GOOD HEDGE AGAINST INFLATION?*
by Homer Hoyt

Dr. Hoyt, the dean of American real estate economists, wrote the following article in 1974 at the age of seventy-nine. He has graciously given permission to reprint it here. He has carried out many studies of land and is the author of much about other facets of real estate. His many articles have been compiled in an 848-page book, *According to Hoyt, 53 Years of Homer Hoyt, 1916–1969.* He is also the author of the classic *One Hundred Years of Land Values in Chicago* (University of Chicago Press, 1933), and with Arthur M. Weimer and George F. Bloom co-author of *"Real Estate"* (Ronald Press, 6th ed., 1972). In his published works, Dr. Hoyt not only has something to say, but he says it very well indeed.

    1. The investor in vacant land that yields no income from farming, timber or minerals must have sufficient annual income from his business or other sources to pay the real estate taxes, interest and

*Copyright © 1974 by Homer Hoyt. (First published in different form under the title *Investment in Vacant Urban Land As a Hedge Against Inflation*, in *The MGIC Newsletter*, November-December 1974, by the MGIC Investment Company.)

principal on the mortgage on the land, which will yield no income until sold. It is usually difficult to borrow on vacant land as security. John Jacob Astor and Marshall Field made fortunes in vacant land investment in the path of city growth because they had large incomes from their business (Astor in the fur trade and Marshall Field in his department store) which enabled them to hold vacant land until it was in demand for building.

2. An interim use for vacant land, such as farming or temporary structures seldom yields a return sufficient to cover real estate taxes, interest and mortgage payments.

3. The holding period may last for ten or twenty years or longer. There is no definite time period for holding that can be relied on. No one should buy on the expectation that the land will increase in value at a constant annual rate. It may have no increase for many years and then suddenly double or triple or even increase tenfold in a year when zoning is secured or a new highway or sewer and water are made available.

4. The investor should seek land in metropolitan areas with potential for rapid growth in basic employment and in those sections of the metropolitan area in the sector with greatest possibility of growth.

5. The only reason for any increase in value of land held for urban growth is the actual utilization of the site on a basis that will produce a net income for the land after deducting interest, depreciation and maintenance of the improvements. The investor in vacant land who does not have sufficient income to maintain the expenses of real estate taxes, interest and principal payments on the mortgage will have the property foreclosed and will lose all of the money he has invested and may be subject to personal liability for the balance of the payments. Vacant land that will never yield an income in the foreseeable future may have no justified value even in times of inflation. It is necessary to estimate how long a period of time must elapse before the land can be utilized for urban development.

6. Speculation may increase sales prices of land above justified levels, as depression may lower them below these levels, but these elements cannot be relied on for investment purposes.

7. There is, even in densely settled metropolitan areas, more land than can ever be absorbed by housing, shopping centers, office buildings and industries. The densely settled urbanized areas of the

United States occupy *only 2 percent* of the land area. Even including scattered houses in metropolitan areas beyond the urbanized areas the total area in which there are any urban dwellings would not exceed 10 percent of the land area of mainland United States, excluding Alaska and Hawaii.

8. Land that yields no income must double in value in six or seven years to equal the return on bonds.

9. Only land should be purchased that has sewer or water available or the prospects of them, or on soil that will percolate.

10. Building of town houses and apartments instead of single family houses lessens the total demand for acreage.

11. Zero population growth lessens the total demand for land.

12. Redevelopment of central cities with building of high-rise apartments near offices will lessen the demand for suburban land.

13. A movement away from large metropolitan centers to smaller towns may become an increasing trend because of air pollution, crime and the long travel time from home to work. This movement will be accelerated in the future by the use of electronic communications devices.

14. Overbuilding of offices, apartments, shopping centers or factories in any given metropolitan area will check demand for land for new building of these facilities.

15. No-growth policies of some cities prevent future building in these areas.

16. Ecology increases the cost of developing land and lowers the raw-land value.

17. Land development and the demand for vacant land for urban uses is contingent upon availability of credit for construction of houses, apartments, shopping centers and office buildings, which are financed by borrowed funds. Long-term credit is available when inflation and rising prices are not rampant. In certain times of depression or restricted credit, little or no mortgage money will be available for new construction.

18. Purchasers of vacant land or improved real estate, unlike buyers of stocks and bonds, assume title risks they do not incur in investing in securities. The delivery of a deed to the buyer of real estate conveys only the title that the seller has, which may be subject to liens, easements, claims or unknown heirs and adverse possession of people who may happen to be living on the land. The description

of the property in the deed must be verified by a survey or it may convey property in a different location from the property the investor thinks he is buying. Title insurance may cover some of these risks but not all of them.

19. The largest profits in land are often secured by the land developer, who prepares development plans, puts in streets, water and sewer connections, secures permits for building by appearing before city or county governing bodies and by organizing a sales campaign to sell houses or improved lots. The investor in land without these connections may obtain only a small part of the gain in the development of raw land. If the original investor in the land subdivides and sells lots himself he may be considered by the Internal Revenue Service to be in the real estate business and any gains he realizes on the sales are taxed as ordinary income and not as capital gains.*

20. I have found in the past that even when the most remarkable bargains in land were offered, such as the Bunker Hill development in the center of downtown Los Angeles and in land along the Gulf of Mexico adjoining Naples, Florida, no large institutional investors could be secured to make the purchases. There is a ready market available for office buildings, shopping centers or apartments that produce a net income but there is no national or even local market by banks, institutions or large investors for vacant land without an income on the fringe of urban areas. There are so many diverse conditions affecting every metropolitan area in the United States, not only with respect to population growth, attitudes of local zoning officials and ecologists, and the vast differences between neighborhoods and communities in the same metropolitan area, that it is necessary for an investor to acquire an expert knowledge of any given property before making an investment. The information given by local brokers, appraisers and market analysts whose knowledge may be confined to a particular kind of property or locality may be misleading.

21. The investor in land for urban development or improved real estate must take into account the fact that except in central

*Author's note: Current tax law holds, as this is written in 1974, that you may sell up to four subdivided lots in a year for your long-term profits to qualify as a capital gain. Sell five or more and your profits are taxed as ordinary income. See chapter 14.

blighted areas occupied mainly by black population, land and building values have been rising steadily since 1934 as a result of demand
and inflation and that we may be at the peak at this time. In the event
of a drastic recession all these values may decline even with inflation.

22. Land advertised as vacation resorts in areas far from existing
cities as well as lands for residential purposes in or near cities may
result in great losses to investors. Any program for land investment
that is widely advertised usually produces great profits to the promoters but often no profit or even losses to the small investor.

23. Local real estate men or public officials may have inside
knowledge of some new highway, sewer system or some zoning
change which they take advantage of but do not reveal to the
general public. The owner of land in the path of these developments, if he lives at a distance from the property, may not learn
of these impending changes and may sell his land too cheap, not
realizing the profit which he otherwise would have gained. These
tracts of land are called "sleepers" where a real estate broker will
rush in and buy the property from an owner who has no knowledge of the impending changes which would greatly increase the
value of his land.

24. If there is rapid inflation in the United States, all improved real estate with rental income not subject to rent control
would rise in value and keep pace with inflation, as would vacant
land needed for new building. However, land with no prospect of
urban use and with zero income, would not necessarily keep pace
with inflation.

25. Bargains in land often require substantial sums of money to
acquire large tracts and these are beyond the financial resources of
small investors. Purchases of small lots from developers or as members of syndicates do not offer the same opportunity for profit.

Conclusion: There are so many pitfalls and risks to be taken into
account in the purchase of vacant land to be held for urban development that the investor may lose or fail to gain more than he could
by putting his money on interest in a savings institution or in buying
bonds, that it is questionable whether the purchase of land to be held
for urban uses is a desirable mode of investment for persons without
independent income and a special knowledge of all the risks and the
prospects of growth for any given type of land in some particular

metropolitan area. A person considering buying vacant land for future urban development is confronted with such a bewildering mass of advertising and offerings by brokers and land owners that it is difficult to make a decision as to which particular parcel offers the best opportunity for profit.

appendix B

LIMITED PARTNERSHIP AGREEMENT

Here is a sample limited partnership agreement that has been used in one form or another in New York State to syndicate land worth up to about $100,000.

The sample agreement that follows is not a rigid, standard form. It has been continually modified and changed according to such variables as the investors buying units in each deal. This agreement is for use in New York State though the land itself may be located elsewhere. If this agreement is used as a model in another state, care should be taken and necessary changes made, of course, to conform with the investment law in the state in which it is used. A check also should be made on any parts of the following agreement that may require modification or changes as a result of legal requirements that came into being after this agreement was written. It is published here mainly to give you an idea of the different kinds of protective clauses and other items to have included when you enter into a land-buying agreement.

WITNESSETH:

WHEREAS, the parties hereto desire to form a limited partnership in accordance with the laws of the State of New York and to acquire for such partnership the ownership of the properties described in Exhibit A attached hereto;

NOW, THEREFORE, it is mutually agreed as follows:

1. *Name and Business:* The parties hereto hereby form a limited partnership pursuant to the provisions of Article 8 of the Partnership Law of the State of New York to acquire the title to the undeveloped properties described in Exhibit A hereto (hereinafter called the "Property"), to hold said Property for investment, and to manage, develop and improve, mortgage, lease, exchange, sell or otherwise transfer or deal with said Property, subject to any restrictions hereinafter imposed under this Agreement, and to engage in all business activities necessary, convenient, incidental or appurtenant to the foregoing purposes.

The name of the partnership shall be _____ and the principal office of the business shall be at _____ or such other place as the General Partners may from time to time determine.

2. *Term:* The term of the partnership shall begin on   and shall continue until   , provided, however, that the partnership shall be dissolved prior to said date upon (a) any disposition by the partnership, other than to a nominee, of its entire interest in all of the Property, including any mortgage or leasehold interest which may be acquired by the partnership in exchange therefor, or (b) the death, retirement, resignation, bankruptcy, expulsion or adjudication of insanity or incompetency of any individual General Partner unless the partnership is continued pursuant to the provisions of paragraph 16 hereof.

3. *Capital Contribution—General Partners:*

(a) _____ shall be the General Partners.

(b) The General Partners shall contribute an aggregate of $100 to the capital of the partnership pro rata in proportion to their respective interests in the Unit held by them, as set forth in paragraph 4 hereof.

4. *Partnership Interests:* The ownership of the partnership shall consist of ten Units, of which the General Partners shall own one (which shall be divided in the following percentages: ____ %, and ____ %,) and the Limited Partners shall own an aggregate of nine Units, all as described in paragraph 5 hereof.

5. *Capital Contributions—Limited Partners,*
   Admission of Additional Limited Partners:

(a) _____ shall be the Initial Limited Partner and shall, upon demand of the General Partners, contribute to the capital of the partnership $100.00 in cash.

(b) The General Partners are authorized to admit to the partnership at such times as the General Partners may deem appropriate additional limited partners who shall contribute to the capital of the partnership sums aggregating not less than $ nor more than $

The total interest in the partnership to be acquired by the additional limited partners shall be divided into nine Units, each representing a contribution of $ to the capital of the partnership (the "Units"). All additional limited partners shall become parties hereto by confirming, approving and adopting this Agreement by executing either personally or by an attorney-in-fact, a conformed counterpart of this Agreement at the foot thereof below the words "Confirmed, Approved and Adopted" and such other documents as the General Partners may require to bind such additional limited partners to all of the terms and provisions of this Agreement, as the same may, from time to time, be amended or modified and by inserting either personally or by an attorney-in-fact below the words "Number of Units Acquired" and "Amount of Capital Contribution" on such conformed copy of this Agreement, the number of Units acquired by such additional limited partner and the amount of said limited partner's capital contribution. Such confirmation, approval and adoption by any additional limited partner shall be binding on the partnership only if accepted by a General Partner in writing on said conformed copy below the signature of the additional limited partner. The original of this Agreement executed by the parties hereto and any executed counterparts thereof and the statements of confirmation, approval and adoption, duly executed and accepted as aforementioned, along with the statements as to the number of Units acquired and amount of capital contribution, taken together, shall constitute a single instrument. To accomplish the purposes of this subparagraph, the General Partners are authorized to do all things necessary to effectuate the admission of such additional limited partners, including, but not limited to, the filing of an amendment or amendments to the Certificate of Limited Partnership of the partnership, reflecting such admissions.

(c) Upon the admission to the partnership of one or more additional limited partners pursuant to subparagraph (b) above, _____ agrees that he shall simultaneously therewith and without the execution of any further documents, be deemed to have withdrawn from the partnership as a limited partner, at which time his cash capital contribution as the Initial Limited Partner of $100.00, if previously paid by him, shall be returned to him and his interests in capital, profits and losses shall be reallocated equally among the nine Units. Accordingly, from and after the date of the admission of one or more additional limited partners pursuant to subparagraph (b) above, the term "Limited Partner" shall be deemed to refer to each individual limited partner admitted pursuant to said subparagraph (b) and the term "Limited Partners" shall be deemed to refer to all of the limited partners admitted pursuant to said subparagraph (b).

(d) Each Limited Partner shall simultaneously with the execution of this Agreement make an initial cash capital contribution of $ per Unit to the partnership. Said initial capital contributions shall be used in connection with the acquisition of the Property, the expenses attendant thereto including sums referred to in paragraph 9 hereof and/or to reimburse the General Partners to the extent they have paid certain funds toward the acquisition of the Property or have advanced monies to defray expenses incurred in connection with the acquisition of the Property.

(e) The Limited Partners shall also contribute from time to time, upon ten (10) days' prior written notice to them by a General Partner, any additional funds needed by the partnership to meet partnership obligations including but not limited to a pro rata portion of (i) the interest and principal payments required under the mortgages on the Property; (ii) real estate and other taxes on the Property, and (iii) the fees payable to the General Partners and the Manager (as hereinafter defined), and expenses incurred or to be incurred by the partnership, such pro rata portion to be computed in accordance with the ratio between (a) each Limited Partner's interest in the partnership and (b) the aggregate of all such Limited Partners' interests. All checks representing payment of capital contributions to the partnership shall be made payable to the partnership, and shall be held by the partnership in its bank account, on behalf of the partnership. All Limited Partners shall periodically receive reports from the partnership as to the amounts so held on deposit and expenditures made on behalf of the partnership.

6. *Default by Limited Partner in Making Capital Contribution:*

(a) In the event any Limited Partner fails to pay any installment of his capital contribution required under Paragraph 5 on or prior to the time therefor set forth herein, he shall be deemed to be in default hereunder (the "Defaulting Limited Partner"). Upon the occurrence of such default, a General Partner shall give notice of such default to all Limited Partners ("Default Notice") specifying the nature of the default and the aggregate capital contributions theretofore contributed by such Defaulting Limited Partner. The nondefaulting Limited Partners shall have the option to purchase each Defaulting Limited Partner's entire interest as Limited Partner, including all profits, losses and distributions attributable to such interest which have not been previously distributed or allocated in a tax return filed by the partnership. Such option may be exercised by a Limited Partner (the "Purchasing Limited Partner") by mailing to the partnership within fifteen (15) days of the mailing of the Default Notice, written notice of his desire to purchase all or parts of each Defaulting Limited Partner's interest as a Limited Partner (the "Purchase Notice") specifying the percentage which the Purchasing Limited Partner desires to purchase. Whether or not this option is exercised, the Defaulting Limited Partner shall thereafter have no right to receive such profits, losses and distributions but any successor to his interest shall receive the benefits of the same.

(b) In the event one or more Purchasing Limited Partners desire to purchase all or part of such Defaulting Limited Partner's interest as a Limited Partner and the total of the percentages they desire to purchase (the "Total Percentage") is equal to or less than the total of such interest of such Defaulting Limited Partner, each Purchasing Limited Partner shall be allowed to purchase the percentage specified in the Purchase Notice on the terms listed below. If any part of such interest is not so purchased by Purchasing Limited Partners, then the General Partners or either of them shall have the option to so purchase on the same terms and conditions, such remaining part of such interest of the Defaulting Limited Partner and to the extent so purchased, they shall be a Limited Partner.

(c) The Purchase Notice shall state that in the event two or more Purchasing Limited Partners desire to purchase a Total Percentage greater than the interest as a Limited Partner of the Defaulting Limited Partner, each shall be entitled to purchase portions of such interest based on the ratio which his respective capital contribution bears to the capital contribution of all the Purchasing Limited Partners. Any Purchasing Limited Partner shall become a substitute

Limited Partner to the extent of any portion of any interest as a Limited Partner which they, or any of them, may purchase hereunder.

(d) The purchase price to be paid to the Defaulting Limited Partner shall be an amount of cash equal to the balance of the capital account (as distinguished from the capital contribution) of the Defaulting Limited Partner as reflected on the books and records of the Partnership at the time of the default referred to herein. Each purchaser shall also (i) pay to the partnership his pro rata share of the capital contribution as to which the default occurred and (ii) execute an undertaking to the partnership to pay his pro rata share of any additional installments of capital contribution required to be made by the Defaulting Limited Partner and to assume all other obligations of the Defaulting Limited Partner, if any, to the partnership.

(e) The General Partners may, in their sole discretion, and without further notice, sell, on behalf of the partnership, all or any part of that portion of the Unit(s) of the Defaulting Limited Partner which have not been purchased by the Limited Partners or General Partners, in which case the Defaulting Limited Partner shall remain liable for any deficiency in his obligations to the partnership subsequent to the sale and shall be entitled to be credited with only the excess, if any, of the amount realized on such sale over the unsatisfied portion of his obligation to the partnership. The General Partners shall, at their option, cause the partnership to institute an action on any unsatisfied portion of the Defaulting Limited Partner's obligations to the partnership. The Limited Partners by the execution of this Agreement, hereby grant to the General Partners, their successors and assigns, an irrevocable power of attorney which shall be deemed coupled with an interest to sell and assign, in whole or in part, the Unit(s) pursuant to this subdivision, on such terms and conditions and for such consideration as the General Partners or their successor may deem advisable either at public auction or by private sale. However, at least ten (10) days' written notice of such sale shall be given to any Defaulting Limited Partner, which notice the parties agree shall be deemed reasonable.

(f) The obligations of a Defaulting Limited Partner to the partnership shall not be extinguished by the existence of any option to purchase, or by its exercise, but only by, and to the extent of, any cash capital contribution made in the Defaulting Limited Partner's place by any partner or partners who have purchased all or any portion of his Unit(s), or any proceeds from the sale of his Unit(s) as aforesaid.

(g) If the option given hereunder shall not be exercised within the foregoing periods, until such default shall be cured, any distributions in respect of the interest of the Defaulting Limited Partner shall be applied first to interest on the defaulted amount at the maximum legal rate and then to the defaulted amount, and the profits and losses in respect thereof shall be allocated to the General Partners.

7. *Profits, Losses and Distributions:*

(a) The net profits and net losses of the partnership for income tax purposes and otherwise shall be allocated among the partners pro rata in proportion to their respective contributions to the capital of the partnership, except that until the partnership has distributed to the Limited Partners an aggregate amount of cash, on a cumulative basis, equal to their capital contributions to the partnership, all net profits and net losses shall be allocated to the Limited Partners.

(b) The General Partners may at such times as the General Partners deem appropriate, distribute to the partners, general and limited, that portion of the partnership's cash funds which the General Partners, in the sole discretion of the General Partners, determine is not needed for partnership operations, reserves or contingencies and is available for distribution. Such distributions shall be made to the partners pro rata in proportion to their respective contributions to the capital of the Partnership except that no cash shall be distributed to the General Partners until the partnership has distributed to the Limited Partners an aggregate amount, on a cumulative basis equal to their capital contributions to the partnership.

(c) The contributions to the capital of the partnership may be returned to the Limited Partners, in whole or in part, at any time in the absolute discretion of the General Partners, provided, however, that such returns of contributions to capital shall be pro rata to all Limited Partners in proportion to their respective contributions to the capital of the partnership.

(d) Notwithstanding anything to the contrary herein contained, the liability of any of the Limited Partners for the losses of the partnership shall in no event exceed in the aggregate the amount of their required contributions and loans to the capital of the partnership. In no event shall the Limited Partners be required to make capital contributions to the partnership in excess of an aggregate of $ per Unit. Any loss in excess of such amount shall be borne solely by the General Partners.

8. *Management, Duties and Restrictions:* During the continuance of this partnership, the rights and liabilities of the General Partners and Limited Partners, respectively, shall be as follows:

(a) *General Partners:*

(i) The General Partners shall have equal rights in the management of the partnership business and shall devote so much of their time to the business of the partnership as shall be reasonably required. The General Partners shall have the exclusive right and power to manage and operate the partnership and to do all things necessary, in their sole discretion, to carry on the business of the partnership, as described in paragraph 1 hereof. It is understood that the General Partners, in their sole discretion, may apply any funds received from a partial sale of the Partnership Property toward payment of the principal and interest on any mortgage of any Partnership Property or payment of the fees and expenses of operating the partnership, or toward further development of any part of the Property of the partnership.

(ii) The General Partners, or either of them, shall have the right, but shall not be obligated, to lend funds to the partnership, from time to time, as the partnership shall, in the discretion of the General Partners require additional funds. Loans by the General Partners shall bear interest at a rate to be determined solely by the General Partners but not in excess of the then predominant prime rate in New York City. Such loans and all accrued interest therein shall be repaid at such times as the General Partners may deem appropriate out of the partnership's available cash funds.

(b) *Limited Partners.* No Limited Partner shall participate in the management of the partnership business in his capacity as a Limited Partner. A Limited Partner shall have the right to withdraw his capital contribution upon the termination of the partnership as provided herein, provided, however, that no part of the capital contribution of any Limited Partner shall be withdrawn unless all liabilities of the partnership except liabilities of the partnership to partners on account of their contributions have been paid or unless the partnership has assets sufficient to pay them. Except as otherwise provided in paragraph 18 hereof, no Limited Partner shall have the right to demand or receive property other than cash in return for this contribution. No Limited Partner shall have priority over any other Limited Partner either as to contributions to capital or as to compensation by way of income.

(c) The Limited Partners hereby consent to any sale or other disposition, encumbrance, mortgage or lease (or modification, cancellation or replacement of any existing mortgage or lease) by the General Partners on behalf of the partnership, of any or all of the partnership's assets on such terms and conditions as may be determined by the General Partners in their sole discretion, and to the employment, when and if required, of such brokers, accountants, managing and other agents and attorneys as the General Partners may from time to time determine. The fact that a partner, general or limited, or a member of his family or an affiliate of any of the foregoing persons is employed by, or directly or indirectly interested in or connected with, any person, firm or corporation employed by the partnership to render or perform a service, or from which the partnership may purchase any property, or to which the Partnership may sell any property, shall not prohibit the General Partners from employing such person, firm or corporation, or from otherwise dealing with him or it, and neither the partnership nor any of the partners herein shall have any rights in or to any income or profits derived therefrom as a consequence of the partnership relationship herein created. It is presently understood that a corporation, in which one or both of the General Partners are principals will manage the Property of the partnership (the "Manager").

(d) Any of the partners, general or limited, may engage in and/or possess an interest in other business ventures of every nature and description independently or with others, including but not limited to the ownership, financing, leasing, operation, management or development of real property and neither the partnership nor any of its partners thereof shall have any rights by virtue of this Agreement in and to said independent ventures or the income or profits derived therefrom.

9. *Compensation, Drawings and Interest on Capital Contributions:* Except as expressly set forth herein, no salaries, compensation or drawings for services rendered on behalf of the partnership shall

be paid to any partner, nor shall any partner receive any interest on his contributions to the capital of the partnership. The General Partners, upon the execution hereof, shall receive a management fee for their services to the partnership of $ and reimbursement for their expenditures on behalf of the partnership to date (not to exceed $). The Manager shall receive $ compensation in the second full fiscal year of the partnership. In addition, all disbursements (not to exceed $600.00 per annum) of the Manager and its employees and agents, expended in connection with the management of the Property shall be repaid to the Manager out of partnership funds.

10. *Banking:* All funds of the partnership shall be deposited in its name in such checking account or accounts as shall be designated by the General Partners. All withdrawals therefrom are to be made by checks signed by one or both of the General Partners as the General Partners shall determine.

11. *Lease, Encumbrances and Conveyances:* Any lease, mortgage, deed, contract of sale or other commitment purporting to convey or encumber the interest of the partnership in all or any portion of the Property held in its name, or any instrument amending or modifying any existing lease, mortgage or commitment, shall be signed by either General Partner and no other signature shall be required.

12. *Books and Tax Returns:* The partnership shall maintain full and accurate books at its principal office and all partners shall have the right to inspect and examine such books at reasonable times at the office of the General Partners. The books shall be closed and balanced at the end of each calendar year, a year-end financial statement prepared by a certified public accountant designated by the General Partners shall be delivered to each Limited Partner, together with a copy of the tax returns which are to be filed for the partnership for the year as to which the statement relates.

13. *Transfer of Units:*

(a) Subject to the provisions of subparagraph (b) below, each Limited Partner shall have the right to assign the whole or any portion of his interest in the profits and losses of the partnership by a written assignment to a person approved in writing by the General Partners, which approval shall not be unreasonably withheld, provided that (i) such assignment contains an affidavit of good title and an

assumption by the assignee of the obligations of the assignor hereunder, and has been duly executed and acknowledged by the assigner
and assignee on an instrument approved by the General Partners, (ii)
a reasonable transfer fee has been paid to the partnership at least
sufficient to cover all reasonable expenses connected with any such
assignment, and (iii) the assignee executes a written statement con-
taining an investment undertaking similar to that set forth in paragraph 14 hereof and stating that the assignee meets any federal or
applicable state suitability standards, such statement to be satisfactory to the General Partners in form and substance. No assignment
of all or any portion of a Limited Partner's interest shall be valid
unless made pursuant to all of the requirements of this Agreement.

(b) Notwithstanding subparagraph (a) above, (i) no interest in
the partnership may be assigned if such interest, when added to the
total of all other interests assigned, sold or exchanged within the
period of 12 consecutive months prior thereto, might result in the
termination of the partnership under Section 708 of the Internal
Revenue Code or the corresponding provision of any subsequent
Federal tax laws and (ii) any such assignment shall be subject to and
contingent upon compliance with any restrictions on transferability
provided by law, including the Securities Act of 1933, as amended,
state laws and the respective rules and regulations promulgated
thereunder.

(c) No Limited Partner shall have the right to substitute an
assignee as a substituted Limited Partner in his place, except with
the prior written consent of the General Partners, which consent
may be withheld for any reason whatsoever in the sole discretion of
the General Partners.

14. *Investment Representation:* Each of the Limited Partners
hereby represents that he is acquiring his Unit(s) hereunder for his
own account and for investment purposes only and not with a view
to further resale, transfer, assignment or distribution thereof in
whole or in part.

15. *Power of Attorney:*

(a) Each of the Limited Partners irrevocably constitutes and
appoints the General Partners, and each of them with full power of
substitution, his true and lawful attorney, for him and his name, place
and stead and for his use and benefit to sign and acknowledge, file
and record all documents necessary to the formation, continuation

and operation of the partnership, including, but not limited to:

(i) The Certificate of Limited Partnership of the partnership and any amendments or modifications to the Certificate of Limited Partnership under applicable laws.

(ii) All forms, reports, documents or other instruments and certificates which may be required or requested of the partnership by any agency or commission of the federal, or any state or local government or by any law or administrative requirement thereof, in which the partnership may sell interests in the partnership, acquire properties or do business, which the General Partners deem advisable and in the best interests of the partnership.

(iii)Any documents which may be required to effect the continuation of the partnership, the admission of any additional or substituted limited partner, or the dissolution and termination of the partnership.

(iv)To make certain elections contained in the Internal Revenue Code of 1954, as amended, or under relevant state law governing taxation of partnerships.

(b) The foregoing power of attorney is a special power of attorney, is irrevocable and shall survive the death or incompetence of the Limited Partner.

16. *Death, Retirement, Resignation, Bankruptcy, Insanity, Expulsion of a General Partner(s).*

(a) In the event of the death, retirement, resignation, bankruptcy, expulsion or adjudication of insanity of a General Partner, the partnership shall be dissolved and terminated, provided, however, the partnership may be continued if the remaining General Partner so elects in accordance with subparagraph (b) below. If the remaining General Partner shall determine to continue the partnership, the withdrawing General Partner or his personal representative shall become a Limited Partner in the partnership.

(b) The remaining General Partner shall determine whether to continue the partnership no later than sixty (60) days following the death, retirement, resignation, bankruptcy, expulsion or adjudication of insanity of the other General Partner, and shall, within said sixty (60) days give written notice of such determination to the Limited Partners.

(c) In the event that the remaining General Partner elects to continue the partnership, the withdrawing General Partner or personal representative of a deceased or incompetent General Partner shall become a Limited Partner in the partnership with the same relative interest in the partnership profits and losses and partnership capital as previously possessed by said General Partner in this partnership, subject, however, to the limitation of liability with respect to future partnership losses to an amount equal to the capital account of said partner as of the date said partner became a Limited Partner hereunder.

17. *Death of a Limited Partner.* The death of a Limited Partner shall not dissolve nor terminate the partnership. In the event of such death, the personal representative of the deceased Limited Partner shall have all the rights of the Limited Partner in the partnership to the extent of the deceased's interest therein, subject to the terms and conditions of the Agreement.

18. *Termination.*

(a) The partnership may be terminated by the General Partners prior to the end of its term after at least thirty (30) days' prior written notice by the General Partners to each of the Limited Partners.

(b) In the event of any dissolution and termination of the partnership, the then General Partners shall proceed to the liquidation of the partnership and the proceeds of such liquidation shall be applied and distributed in the following order of priority:

(i) To the payment of the debts and liabilities of the partnership (other than any loans or advances that may have been made by the partners to the partnership) and the expenses of liquidation.

(ii) To the setting up of any reserves which the General Partners may deem reasonably necessary for any contingent or unforeseen liabilities or obligations of the partnership or of the General Partners arising out of or in connection with the partnership. Said reserves shall be paid over by the General Partners to an Escrowee satisfactory to a majority of the Limited Partners and General Partners, to be held by him for the purpose of disbursing such reserves in payment of any of the aforementioned contingencies, and, at the expiration of such period, as the General Partners shall deem advisable, to distribute the balance thereafter remaining in the manner hereinafter provided.

(iii)To the repayment, pro rata, of any loans or advances that may have been made by any of the partners to the partnership.

(iv)Any balance remaining shall be distributed among all partners, both general and limited, in the same proportions as profits and losses are shared pursuant to this Agreement.

(c) Each of the Partners shall be furnished with a statement prepared by the partnership's then certified public accountants, which shall set forth the assets and liabilities of the partnership as at the date of complete liquidation.

(d) Upon the General Partner's complying with the foregoing distribution plan (including payment over by the Escrowee if there are sufficient funds therefor), the Limited Partners shall cease to be such, and the General Partners, as the sole remaining partners of the partnership, shall execute, acknowledge and cause to be filed a Certificate of Cancellation of the partnership.

(e) Anything in this agreement to the contrary notwithstanding, the General Partners shall not be personally liable for the return of the capital contributions of Limited Partners, or any portion thereof, it being expressly understood that any such return shall be made solely from partnership assets.

19. *Indemnity.* The partnership shall indemnify and hold harmless the General Partners and the Manager from any loss or damage incurred by them or either of them (including attorneys' fees and expenses) by reason of any act performed or not performed by them or either of them for and on behalf of the partnership and in furtherance of its interests. The doing of any act or failure to do any act by the General Partners or the Manager, the effect of which may cause or result in loss or damage to the partnership shall not subject the General Partners or the Manager or their successors and assigns to any liability unless the General Partners or the Manager shall be adjudicated guilty of fraud or gross negligence.

20. *Signing.* Each of the Limited Partners expressly understands that the figures submitted to him in the proposals by the General Partners as to costs of acquisition could be subject to change following possible changes in acreage as a result of surveys or others, adjustments and final costs as determined by closing statements. Each of the Limited Partners will sign the Agreement when submitted to him to avoid cumbersome mailings of the Agreement after the closings for the Property. The Limited Partners will be advised of any higher or lower costs by the General Partners and shall be billed accordingly. Because the General Partners are diligent in trying to

determine the full costs when negotiating the purchase of the Property, it is the firm belief that the changes, if any, will be small, but the General Partners make no representation or warranty as to the size of such changes.

21. *Amendment, Binding, etc.* This Agreement may be amended only by unanimous written consent of all partners. This Agreement shall be construed in accordance with the laws of the State of New York, shall be binding upon and inure to the benefit of all parties, their personal representatives, successors and assigns, and may be executed in any number of counterparts, each of which so executed shall be deemed to be an original.

22. *Action of General Partners.* The partnership shall be bound only by action taken or documents executed by the General Partners or either of them.

23. *Notices.* All notices provided for in this Agreement shall be directed to the partners at the addresses herein set forth and to the partnership at its principal office by Registered or Certified Mail or to such other address as the party to whom such notice is due shall have previously given written notice to the other partners to this Agreement.

IN WITNESS WHEREOF, the parties hereto have hereunto set their hands and seals as of the day and year first above written.

General Partners:

_____

_____

Initial Limited Partner:

_____

Confirmed, Approved and Adopted	*Limited Partners Number of Units Acquired*	*Amount of Capital Contribution*
1. _____	_____	$

Accepted: _____
, A General Partner

2. _____ _____ $

   Accepted: _____
                   , A General Partner

3. _____ _____ $

   Accepted: _____
                   , A General Partner

4. _____ _____ $

   Accepted: _____
                   , A General Partner

5. _____ _____ $

   Accepted: _____
                   , A General Partner

State of New York   )
                         ss.:
County of   —,)

    On the   day of   , 19 , before me personally came
      , to me known to be the individual described in and who
executed the foregoing instrument, and acknowledged that he executed the same.

                              _____

State of New York   )
                         ss.:
County of   )

    On the   day of   , 19 , before me personally came
      , to me known to be the individual described in and who
executed the foregoing instrument, and acknowledged that he executed the same.

                              _____

BIBLIOGRAPHY

Here is a listing of books which the author has found helpful plus other books by this author on related subjects.

According to Hoyt–53 years of Homer Hoyt, 1916–1969. $12.50 postpaid; Homer Hoyt Institute, 2939 Van Ness Street N.W., Washington, D.C. 20008. A compilation of Dr. Hoyt's writings on ". . . the law, real estate cycle, economic base, sector theory, shopping centers, urban growth" and other subjects. Virtually essential reading for any real student of the subject.

Buying Country Land, by Eugene Boudreau; 1973. $4.95; The Macmillan Company, 100K Brown Street, Riverside, N.J. 08075. An excellent little book, easy to read, with much helpful information about legal considerations, and especially on evaluating land for water supply and sewage disposal.

Buying Country Property, by Herb Moral; 1973. $3; Bantam Books, 414 E. Golf Road, Des Plaines, Ill. 60016. Chiefly concerned with buying a house in the country and how to evaluate the house.

Handbook of Real Estate Investment, by Don G. Campbell; 1968. $7.50; Bobbs-Merrill Co., 4300 West 62nd Street, Indianapolis, Ind. 46268. A wide ranging book on many facets of the subject, written by a leading journalist and financial columnist.

The Land Game, by Albert Winnikoff; 1970, $3; Wilshire Books, 12015 Sherman Road, N. Hollywood, Cal. 91605. Much practical information on buying land for investment, avoiding pitfalls, plus interesting case histories by a man who speaks from nearly 20 years experience doing it himself.

Land Speculation: An evaluation and analysis by Harry L. Oppenheimer; 1972. $9.95; The Interstate Printers and Publishers, Inc. Danville, Ill. 61832. This is mainly for the reader interested in buying a cattle ranch or grazing land. It contains some excellent background and history about the founding of the great ranches ("the big spreads") of the American West. The author is the head of a large national real estate firm specializing in ranchland with head-quarters in Kansas City, Missouri.

Principles of City Land Values, or *The Rise of Urban America* by Richard M. Hurd; 1904; reprinted in 1970. $8; Arno Press, 330 Madison Ave., New York, N.Y. 10017. A classic book on the formation of cities, especially in the United States, and the influences on land and property values. Also essential reading, for any student of the subject.

Questions and Answers on Real Estate by Robert W. Semenow; 7th edition, 1972. $9.95; Prentice-Hall, Inc., Englewood Cliffs, N.J. 07632. A perennial best seller in the real estate field with questions about common happenings in the buying and selling of real estate; much emphasis on legal questions.

Suburban Land Conversion in the United States: An Economic and Governmental Process by Marion Clawson, 1971. $12.50; Johns Hopkins Press, Baltimore, Md. 21218. A comprehensive scholarly work by one of the nation's leading authorities on land.

Other books on related subjects by the author.

Each of the following can be obtained by mail from All About Houses, Piermont, N.Y. 10968. Include 35 cents per book for postage and handling.

How to Avoid the 10 Biggest Home-Buying Traps by A.M. Watkins; 1972 $2.95; Hawthorn Books, Inc. Tells how to avoid the most common pitfalls and traps encountered when you build or buy a house and, as a result, get a good house. Contains a homebuying checklist which is "invaluable," says *Harper's* Magazine.

How to Judge a House by A.M. Watkins; 1972, $1.95; Hawthorn Books, Inc. A pocket guide designed to give a fast and clear presentation of important facts about buying a house.

The Home-Owner's Survival Kit by A.M. Watkins; 1971, $2.95; Hawthorn Books, Inc. How to beat the high cost of owning and operating a house with special chapters on reducing energy bills for monthly utilities, heating and cooling.

INDEX

207